A
HIDDEN
WHOLENESS

A
HIDDEN
WHOLENESS

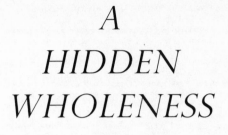

The Journey Toward
an
Undivided Life

Welcoming the soul
and weaving community
in a wounded world

PARKER J. PALMER

JOSSEY-BASS
A Wiley Imprint
www.josseybass.com

Published by Jossey-Bass
A Wiley Imprint
989 Market Street, San Francisco, CA 94103-1741 —www.josseybass.com

Library of Congress Cataloging-in-Publication Data
Palmer, Parker J.
  A hidden wholeness : the journey toward an undivided life / Parker J. Palmer.— 1st ed.
    p. cm.
  Includes bibliographical references and index.
  ISBN 978-0-7879-7100-7 (alk. paper)
  ISBN 978-0-4704-5376-6 (paperback)
  1. Spiritual life. I. Title.
  BV4501.3.P35 2004
  248.4—dc22   2004006421
Printed in the United States of America
FIRST EDITION
HB Printing 10 9 8 7 6 5
PB Printing 10 9 8 7 6 5 4 3

Contents

FOR MARCY JACKSON AND RICK JACKSON
WITH GRATITUDE AND LOVE

Gratitudes

This book brings together four themes I have been musing on since my mid-twenties: the shape of an integral life, the meaning of community, teaching and learning for transformation, and nonviolent social change.

As six previous books and forty years of lecturing prove, I love to think, talk, and write about these things. But—knowing how quickly words can cut loose from human reality—I love it even more when language comes to life. So I take deep satisfaction in the fact that the most important words in this book have already found embodiment, thanks to the gifted people I am privileged to call colleagues and friends.

In cities across the country, these people have created settings where others can join in "the journey toward an undivided life." They are so numerous I cannot list them by name, but I want to point toward them with gratitude for their caring, competence, and commitment:

- The staff and board of the Fetzer Institute, who have supported so much of the work on which this book is based
- The staff and board of the Center for Teacher Formation, who provide educators and people from many other walks of life

with opportunities to deepen their personal and professional integrity[1]

- The one hundred–plus people and counting in the United States and Canada who have gone through the center's facilitator preparation program, learning how to create "circles of trust" where people can take an inner journey toward living "divided no more"

- The countless educators, philanthropists, physicians, attorneys, businesspeople, community organizers, clergy, and others who participate in such circles because they know their own need, and the world's, for rejoining soul and role

- The staff of Jossey-Bass and John Wiley, who actively support this book, and others related to it, because they believe in the work that it advocates

A few people have made special efforts to help this book and its author along. They all have my gratitude and love:

- Marcy Jackson and Rick Jackson are codirectors of the Center for Teacher Formation. For nearly a decade they have led the effort to create circles of trust in far-flung places, doing so with skill, patience, wisdom, vision, and love. I dedicate this book to them to honor their remarkable work and to let them know again how much their friendship means to me.

- Rob Lehman is president emeritus of the Fetzer Institute and chair of its board of trustees. He has a strong and abiding vision of how vital it is to join the inner and outer life. Without his friendship and encouragement, much of the work on which this book is based might well have remained undone.

- Tom Beech is president of the Fetzer Institute. A much-valued friend since our days as college classmates, he was an early advocate of the local and national work of the Center for Teacher Formation. As long as I have known him, he has modeled the undivided life.

- David Sluyter is a senior adviser to the Fetzer Institute, and Mickey Olivanti is a Fetzer Institute program officer. They helped me launch the teacher formation program in the early 1990s and have supported it faithfully ever since. They are good friends and colleagues whose confidence and companionship mean a great deal to me.[2]

- Mark Nepo, Chip Wood, and Roland Johnson are, respectively, a poet and essayist, a public school principal, and an attorney. They are also good friends and fellow travelers who gave various versions of this manuscript a thoughtful reading, and I am grateful for their generous help.

- Earlene Bond, Ann Faulkner, Guy Gooding, Sue Jones, Elaine Sullivan, and Bill Tucker are leaders in the Dallas County Community College District who have brought formation into their part of the educational world through the Center for Formation in the Community College.[3] I am grateful for their friendship and support.

- David Leach, M.D., executive director of the Accreditation Council for Graduate Medical Education, and Paul Batalden, M.D., professor of pediatrics and community and family medicine at Dartmouth Medical School, are leaders in transforming medical education and health care. They have shown me how the key ideas in this book speak to a profession that I know little about, and I value their encouragement and friendship.[4]

- Sheryl Fullerton is my editor. She is a gifted maker and marketer of books with great wisdom about that arcane craft, as well as a treasured friend who knows when I need consolation and when I need a challenge. I thank her and her talented colleagues at Jossey-Bass and John Wiley who have worked hard to bring this book into being: Joanne Clapp Fullagar, Paula Goldstein, Chandrika Madhavan, Sandy Siegle, and Bruce Emmer.

- Sharon Palmer is my best friend, my most trusted critic, and my love. She is the first reader of everything I write—and since I throw out twenty pages for every one I keep, she does a lot of reading. When I asked her what she looks for when she edits, she answered with three questions: Is it worth saying? Is it said clearly? Is it said beautifully? That should explain both my throw-out ratio and why I need to keep working on my writing.

- We are grateful to the Lilly Endowment, Inc., for their generous support of the production of this Leader's Guide and of the Circles of Trust DVD.

❧

Twenty years ago, during a summer teaching stint in England, I picked up a small volume of poetry in a Cambridge bookstore. In it was a haunting little poem by D. M. Thomas called "Stone," which I copied and put into my briefcase, where it can be found to this day. Thomas muses on the titles of a series of books that "the poet" will write over his or her lifetime and ends with these lines:

> *There is also the seventh book, perhaps, the seventh,*
> *And called The Seventh Book because it is not published,*
> *The one that a child thinks he could have written,*
> *Made of the firmest stone and clearest leaves,*
> *That a people keep alive by, keep alive.*[5]

From the moment I first read "Stone," I sensed that it held a message for me. Last year, when I suddenly realized that *A Hidden Wholeness* would be my seventh book, I began to wonder if the message was that I should not publish it! Some critics may wish that I had come to that conclusion, but obviously I did not.

"Stone" speaks to me, I think, about the hope that has kept me writing for forty years, the hope to find words that might somehow give someone life. I do not know if the words in this book will fulfill that hope. But I do know that the work on which this book is based—the work of bringing people together to rediscover and reclaim their wholeness—has given me more life than anything else I have done professionally. May this book allow more people to benefit as much as I have from the life-giving, world-healing power of communities that welcome the soul.

Prelude

The Blizzard of the World

The blizzard of the world
has crossed the threshold
and it has overturned
the order of the soul.
—LEONARD COHEN[1]

There was a time when farmers on the Great Plains, at the first sign of a blizzard, would run a rope from the back door out to the barn. They all knew stories of people who had wandered off and been frozen to death, having lost sight of home in a whiteout while still in their own backyards.

Today we live in a blizzard of another sort. It swirls around us as economic injustice, ecological ruin, physical and spiritual violence, and their inevitable outcome, war. It swirls within us as fear and frenzy, greed and deceit, and indifference to the suffering of others. We all know stories of people who have wandered off into this madness and been separated from their own souls, losing their moral bearings and even their mortal lives: they make headlines because they take so many innocents down with them.

The lost ones come from every walk of life: clergy and corporate executives, politicians and people on the street, celebrities and schoolchildren. Some of us fear that we, or those we love, will become lost in the storm. Some are lost at this moment and are trying to find the way home. Some are lost without knowing it. And some are using the blizzard as cover while cynically exploiting its chaos for private gain.

So it is easy to believe the poet's claim that "the blizzard of the world" has overturned "the order of the soul," easy to believe that the soul—that life-giving core of the human self, with its hunger for truth and justice, love and forgiveness—has lost all power to guide our lives.

But my own experience of the blizzard, which includes getting lost in it more often than I like to admit, tells me that it is not so. The soul's order can never be destroyed. It may be obscured by the whiteout. We may forget, or deny, that its guidance is close at hand. And yet we are still in the soul's backyard, with chance after chance to regain our bearings.

This book is about tying a rope from the back door out to the barn so that we can find our way home again. When we catch sight of the soul, we can survive the blizzard without losing our hope or our way. When we catch sight of the soul, we can become healers in a wounded world—in the family, in the neighborhood, in the workplace, and in political life—as we are called back to our "hidden wholeness" amid the violence of the storm.

CHAPTER I

Images of Integrity

Living "Divided No More"

Jack pines . . . are not lumber trees [and they] won't win many beauty contests either. But to me this valiant old tree, solitary on its own rocky point, is as beautiful as a living thing can be. . . . In the calligraphy of its shape against the sky is written strength of character and perseverance, survival of wind, drought, cold, heat, disease. . . . In its silence it speaks of . . . wholeness . . . an integrity that comes from being what you are.

—DOUGLAS WOOD[1]

❧ Into the Wilderness ❧

Every summer, I go to the Boundary Waters, a million acres of pristine wilderness along the Minnesota-Ontario border. My first trip, years ago, was a vacation, pure and simple. But as I returned time and again to that elemental world of water, rock, woods, and sky, my vacation began to feel more like a pilgrimage to me—an annual trek to holy ground driven by spiritual need. Douglas Wood's meditation on the jack pine, a tree native to that part of the world, names what I go up north seeking: images of how life looks when it is lived with integrity.

Thomas Merton claimed that "there is in all things . . . a hidden wholeness."[2] But back in the human world—where we are less self-revealing than jack pines—Merton's words can, at times, sound like wishful thinking. Afraid that our inner light will be extinguished or our inner darkness exposed, we hide our true identities from each other. In the process, we become separated from our own souls. We end up living divided lives, so far removed from the truth we hold within that we cannot know the "integrity that comes from being what you are."

My knowledge of the divided life comes first from personal experience: I yearn to be whole, but dividedness often seems the easier choice. A "still, small voice" speaks the truth about me, my work, or the world. I hear it and yet act as if I did not. I withhold a personal gift that might serve a good end or commit myself to a project that I do not really believe in. I keep silent on an issue I should address or actively break faith with one of my own convictions. I deny my inner darkness, giving it more power over me, or I project it onto other people, creating "enemies" where none exist.

I pay a steep price when I live a divided life—feeling fraudulent, anxious about being found out, and depressed by the fact that I am denying my own selfhood. The people around me pay a price as well, for now they walk on ground made unstable by my dividedness. How can I affirm another's identity when I deny my own? How can I trust another's integrity when I defy my own? A fault line runs down the middle of my life, and whenever it cracks open—divorcing my words and actions from the truth I hold within—things around me get shaky and start to fall apart.

But up north, in the wilderness, I sense the wholeness hidden "in all things." It is in the taste of wild berries, the scent of sun-baked pine, the sight of the Northern Lights, the sound of water lapping the shore, signs of a bedrock integrity that is eternal and beyond all doubt. And when I return to a human world that is transient and riddled with disbelief, I have new eyes for the wholeness hidden in me and my kind and a new heart for loving even our imperfections.

In fact, the wilderness constantly reminds me that wholeness is not about perfection. On July 4, 1999, a twenty-minute maelstrom of hurricane-force winds took down twenty million trees across the Boundary Waters.[3] A month later, when I made my annual pilgrimage up north, I was heartbroken by the ruin and wondered whether I wanted to return. And yet on each visit since, I have been astonished to see how nature uses devastation to stimulate new growth, slowly but persistently healing her own wounds.

Wholeness does not mean perfection: it means embracing brokenness as an integral part of life. Knowing this gives me hope that human wholeness—mine, yours, ours—need not be a utopian dream, if we can use devastation as a seedbed for new life.

❧ **Beyond Ethics** ❧

The divided life comes in many and varied forms. To cite just a few examples, it is the life we lead when

- We refuse to invest ourselves in our work, diminishing its quality and distancing ourselves from those it is meant to serve
- We make our living at jobs that violate our basic values, even when survival does not absolutely demand it
- We remain in settings or relationships that steadily kill off our spirits
- We harbor secrets to achieve personal gain at the expense of other people
- We hide our beliefs from those who disagree with us to avoid conflict, challenge, and change
- We conceal our true identities for fear of being criticized, shunned, or attacked

Dividedness is a personal pathology, but it soon becomes a problem for other people. It is a problem for students whose teachers "phone it in" while taking cover behind their podiums and their power. It is a problem for patients whose doctors practice medical indifference, hiding behind a self-protective scientific facade. It is a problem for employees whose supervisors have personnel handbooks where their hearts should be. It is a problem for citizens whose political leaders speak "with forked tongue."

As I write, the media are filled with stories of people whose dividedness is now infamous. They worked at such places as Enron, Arthur Andersen, Merrill Lynch, WorldCom, and the Roman Catholic Church, to name a few. Surely these people heard an inner call to wholeness. But they became separated from their own souls, betraying the trust of citizens, stockholders, and the faithful—and making our democracy, our economy, and our religious institutions less trustworthy in the process.

These particular stories will soon fade from the front page, but the story of the divided life will be in the news forever. Its drama is perennial, and its social costs are immense. The poet Rumi said it with ruthless candor eight hundred years ago: "If you are here unfaithfully with us / you're causing terrible damage."[4]

How shall we understand the pathology of the divided life? If we approach it as a problem to be solved by "raising the ethical bar"—exhorting each other to jump higher and meting out tougher penalties to those who fall short—we may feel more virtuous for a while, but we will not address the problem at its source.

The divided life, at bottom, is not a failure of ethics. It is a failure of human wholeness. Doctors who are dismissive of patients, politicians who lie to the voters, executives who cheat retirees out of their savings, clerics who rob children of their well-being—these people, for the most part, do not lack ethical knowledge or convictions. They doubtless took courses on professional ethics and probably received top grades. They gave speeches and sermons on ethical issues and more than likely believed their own words. But they had a well-rehearsed habit of holding their own knowledge and beliefs at great remove from the living of their lives.

That habit is vividly illustrated by a story in the news as I write. The former CEO of a biotechnology firm was convicted of insider trading and sentenced to seven years in prison after putting his daughter and elderly father in legal jeopardy by having them cover for him. Asked what was on his mind as he committed his crimes, he said, "I could sit there . . . thinking I was the most honest CEO that ever lived [and] at the same time . . . glibly do something [wrong] and rationalize it."[5]

Those words were spoken by an expert at "compartmentalizing"—a much-prized capacity in many lines of work but at bottom no more than a six-syllable name for the divided life. Few of us may share the speaker's fate, but many of us already share his expertise: we developed it at school, where ethics, like most subjects, tends to be taught in ways that leave our inner lives untouched.

As teenagers and young adults, we learned that self-knowledge counts for little on the road to workplace success. What counts is the "objective" knowledge that empowers us to manipulate the world. Ethics, taught in this context, becomes one more arm's-length study of great thinkers and their thoughts, one more exercise in data collection that fails to inform our hearts.

I value ethical standards, of course. But in a culture like ours—which devalues or dismisses the reality and power of the inner life—ethics too often becomes an external code of conduct, an objective set of rules we are told to follow, a moral exoskeleton we put on hoping to prop ourselves up. The problem with exoskeletons is simple: we can slip them off as easily as we can don them.

I also value integrity. But that word means much more than adherence to a moral code: it means "the state or quality of being entire, complete, and unbroken," as in *integer* or *integral.* Deeper still, integrity refers to something—such as a jack pine or the human self—in its "unimpaired, unadulterated, or genuine state, corresponding to its original condition."[6]

When we understand integrity for what it is, we stop obsessing over codes of conduct and embark on the more demanding journey toward being whole. Then we learn the truth of John Middleton Murry's remark, "For the good [person] to realize that it is better to be whole than to be good is to enter on a strait and narrow path compared to which his [or her] previous rectitude was flowery license."[7]

⚜ Living "Divided No More" ⚜

A jack pine "solitary on its rocky point" is one of the loveliest sights I know. But lovelier still is the sight of a man or woman standing with integrity intact. Speak the names of Rosa Parks or Nelson Mandela—or other names known nowhere but within your own grateful heart—and you catch a glimpse of the beauty that arises when people refuse to live divided lives.

Of course, wholeness comes more easily to jack pines than to human beings: *Pinus banksia* is unable to think itself into trouble! We are cursed with the blessing of consciousness and choice, a two-edged sword that both divides us and can help us become whole. But choosing wholeness, which sounds like a good thing, turns out to be risky business, making us vulnerable in ways we would prefer to avoid.

As I was working on this book, *Time* magazine published its 2002 year-end issue, naming Cynthia Cooper, Coleen Rowley, and Sherron Watkins its "Persons of the Year."[8] They were honored for confronting corruption at WorldCom, the FBI, and Enron, respectively, honored for turning their consciousness toward living "divided no more." They took their inner truth into the outer world, reclaiming their personal wholeness and helping our society reclaim some of its own.

Sadly such courage is not universally admired. Sherron Watkins has been reviled by some of her ex-colleagues at Enron, who believe that if she had kept her mouth shut, they could have saved the company and their jobs.[9] Since much of the evidence suggests that Enron had become a massive shell game, their criticism tells us less about a good business plan than about how unpopular integrity can be. "There is a price to be paid," said Cynthia Cooper of WorldCom. "There have been times that I could not stop crying."[10]

In the wash of information that surrounds us, the stories of Cooper, Rowley, and Watkins will soon be swept away. And yet I have to wonder, is information overload our problem, or did we *want* to forget how these three witnessed to the real-world possibility of an undivided life? That three ordinary people refused to live a lie means the rest of us could do it, too—if we were willing to embrace the challenge of becoming whole.

But we cannot embrace that challenge all alone, at least, not for long: we need trustworthy relationships, tenacious communities of support, if we are to sustain the journey toward an undivided life. That journey has solitary passages, to be sure, and yet it is simply too arduous to take without the assistance of others. And because we have such a vast capacity for self-delusion, we will inevitably get lost *en route* without correctives from outside of ourselves.

Over the years, my own need for community has led me to collaborate with others in creating settings where there is mutual encouragement for "rejoining soul and role." One result has been a national retreat program for public school educators who face daily threats to their personal and professional integrity—threats that, if they go unmet, will imperil our children's well-being.[11]

As word of that program spread, people in other arenas—parents and politicians, clergy and physicians, community organizers and corporate executives, youth workers and attorneys—began to ask where they could get similar help. In response, the program was expanded to help people from many walks of life bring their integrity more fully into the world.[12]

So this book is not a theory in search of applications: the principles and practices explored here have been proven on the ground. Now they seek even wider use, wherever people want to live undivided lives that are joined to the needs of the world. The first half of the book explores the sources of our dividedness and of the call to live "divided no more." The second half offers guidance for creating settings where people can support each other on the journey toward an undivided life:

- Chapter II diagnoses the divided life, examines its personal and social consequences, and tells stories of what integrity looks like from infancy into adulthood.

- Chapter III lays out evidence for the claim that we arrive in this world with a soul or true self and looks at what happens when we ignore, defy, or embrace our own truth.

- Chapter IV explores a paradox: our solitary journey toward rejoining soul and role requires relationships, a rare but real form of community that I call a "circle of trust."

- Chapter V names the preparations required if that inner journey in community is to take us somewhere worth going.

- Chapters VI, VII, VIII, and IX describe in detail the practices necessary to create spaces between us where the soul feels safe enough to show up and make its claim on our lives.

- Chapter X makes the case that the principles and practices explored in this book can help us walk the path of nonviolence in our everyday lives. Can we learn to respond to the mounting violence of our time with soul-honoring and life-giving ways of being in the world? Much depends on the answer.

CHAPTER II

Across the Great Divide

Rejoining Soul and Role

As once the wingèd energy of delight
carried you over childhood's dark abysses,
now beyond your own life build the great
arch of unimagined bridges.
—RAINER MARIA RILKE[1]

❧ A Child's Secret Life ☙

The instinct to protect ourselves by living divided lives emerges when we are young, as we start to see the gaps between life's bright promise and its shadowy realities. But as children, we are able to deal with those "dark abysses" by sailing across them on the "wingèd energy of delight" that is every child's birthright gift.

This energy comes from the soul—the core of pure being that children are so intimate with—that is, as the poet Rumi says, "here for its own joy."[2] The remarkable resilience youngsters often reveal, even in the face of great hardship, comes from this place called the soul. And the soul animates the "secret lives" that many of us led as children, in an effort to shield our vulnerable selfhood from the threats of the world.

My own secret life started in the fifth or sixth grade. At school, where I wanted to fit in, people saw me as outgoing and self-assured. I made friends easily, knew how to get a laugh, often had my hand up in class, and was elected president of one thing and another more often than FDR. Though I could not dribble a basketball downcourt without tripping over myself, my clumsiness served me well, making me less threatening to other boys and evoking the maternal instinct in girls.

But no one knew how anxious my public role made me. After school, I did not hang out with friends; I hid out in my bedroom. With the door shut tight against the world, I read stories, built model airplanes, or immersed myself in the fantasy realm of radio serial adventures. My room was a monastic cell where I could be the self with whom I felt most at home—the introspective and imaginative self so unlike the extrovert I played with such anxiety at school.

The details of this story are mine alone, but at bottom it is the story of most people I know. As we cross the rising terrain between infancy and adolescence—still close enough to our origins to be in touch with inner truth but aware of the mounting pressure to play someone else "out there"—the true self starts to feel threatened. We deal with the threat by developing a child's version of the divided life, commuting daily between the public world of role and the hidden world of soul.

The secret lives of children have inspired some splendid literature, of course. In C. S. Lewis's classic *Chronicles of Narnia,* we read about a magic wardrobe through which young Peter, Susan, Edmund, and Lucy pass from their humdrum existence in the English countryside into a parallel universe of light and shadow, of mystery and moral demand, confronting the daunting and bracing challenges of the inner journey.[3] I have never doubted the truth of the Narnia tales: that magic wardrobe was in my bedroom, too!

But when we turn from literature to life, this charming feature of childhood soon disappears, to be replaced by an adult pathology. As the outer world becomes more demanding—and today it presses in on children at an obscenely early age—we stop going to our rooms, shutting the door, walking into the wardrobe, and entering the world of the soul. And the closer we get to adulthood, the more we stifle the imagination that journey requires. Why? Because imagining other possibilities for our lives would remind us of the painful gap between who we most truly are and the role we play in the so-called real world.

As we become more obsessed with succeeding, or at least surviving, in that world, we lose touch with our souls and disappear into our roles. The child with a harmless after-school secret becomes the masked and armored adult—at considerable cost to self, to others, and to the world at large. It is a cost that can be itemized in ways well known to many of us:

- We sense that something is missing in our lives and search the world for it, not understanding that what is missing is us.

- We feel fraudulent, even invisible, because we are not in the world as who we really are.

- The light that is within us cannot illuminate the world's darkness.

- The darkness that is within us cannot be illuminated by the world's light.

- We project our inner darkness on others, making "enemies" of them and making the world a more dangerous place.

- Our inauthenticity and projections make real relationships impossible, leading to loneliness.

- Our contributions to the world—especially through the work we do—are tainted by duplicity and deprived of the life-giving energies of true self.

Those are not exactly the marks of a life well lived. But they are not uncommon among us, in part because the dividedness that creates them comes highly recommended by popular culture. "Don't wear your heart on your sleeve" and "Hold your cards close to your vest" are just two examples of how we are told from an early age that "masked and armored" is the safe and sane way to live.

But our culture has it backward. The truth is that the more dividedness we perceive in each other, the less safe and sane we feel. Every day—as we interact with family, friends, acquaintances, and strangers—we ask ourselves if "what we see is what we get." And all those other people are asking the same about us! Being cautious about the degree of congruence between outer appearance and inner reality is one of our species' most ancient ways of seeking safety in a perilous world.

"Is this person the same on the inside as he or she seems to be on the outside?" Children ask this about their parents, students about their teachers, employees about their supervisors, patients about their physicians, and citizens about their political leaders. When the answer is yes, we relax, believing that we are in the presence of integrity and feeling secure enough to invest ourselves in the relationship and all that surrounds it.

But when the answer is no, we go on high alert. Not knowing who or what we are dealing with and feeling unsafe, we hunker down in a psychological foxhole and withhold the investment of our energy, commitment, and gifts. Students refuse to take the risks involved in learning, employees do not put their hearts into their work, patients cannot partner with physicians in their own healing, and citizens disengage from the political process. The perceived incongruity of inner and outer—the inauthenticity that we sense in others, or they in us—constantly undermines our morale, our relationships, and our capacity for good work.

So "masked and armored," it turns out, is *not* the safe and sane way to live. If our roles were more deeply informed by the truth that is in our souls, the general level of sanity and safety would rise dramatically. A teacher who shares his or her identity with students is more effective than one who lobs factoids at them from behind a wall. A supervisor who leads from personal authenticity gets better work out of people than one who leads from a script. A doctor who invests selfhood in his or her practice is a better healer than one who treats patients at arm's length. A politician who brings personal integrity into leadership helps us reclaim the popular trust that distinguishes true democracy from its cheap imitations.

Becoming Whole Adults

The divided life may be endemic, but wholeness is always a choice. Once I have seen my dividedness, do I continue to live a contradiction—or do I try to bring my inner and outer worlds back into harmony?

"Being whole" is a self-evident good, so the answer would seem to be clear. And yet, as we all know, it is not. Time after time we choose against wholeness by slipping into a familiar pattern of evasion:

- First comes denial: surely what I have seen about myself cannot be true!

- Next comes equivocation: the inner voice speaks softly, and truth is a subtle, slippery thing, so how can I be sure of what my soul is saying?

- Next comes fear: if I let that inner voice dictate the shape of my life, what price might I have to pay in a world that sometimes punishes authenticity?

- Next comes cowardice: the divided life may be destructive, but at least I know the territory, while what lies beyond it is *terra incognita.*

- Then comes avarice: in some situations, I am rewarded for being willing to stifle my soul.

This pattern of self-evasion is powerful and persistent. But here is a real-world story about someone who found the courage to break out of it and embrace his own truth.

It happened at a retreat I facilitated for some twenty elected and appointed officials from Washington, D.C. All of them had gone into government animated by an ethic of public service, all were experiencing painful conflicts between their values and power politics, and all sought support for the journey toward living "divided no more."

One participant had worked for a decade in the U.S. Department of Agriculture, after farming for twenty-five years in northeastern Iowa. On his desk at that moment was a proposal related to the preservation of midwestern topsoil, which is being depleted at a rapid rate by agribusiness practices that value short-term profits over the well-being of the earth. His "farmer's heart," he kept saying, knew how the proposal should be handled. But his political instincts warned him that following his heart would result in serious trouble, not least with his immediate superior.

On the last morning of our gathering, the man from Agriculture, looking bleary-eyed, told us that it had become clear to him during a sleepless night that he needed to return to his office and follow his farmer's heart.

After a thoughtful silence, someone asked him, "How will you deal with your boss, given his opposition to what you intend to do?"

"It won't be easy," replied this farmer-turned-bureaucrat. "But during this retreat, I've remembered something important: I don't report to my boss. I report to the land."

Because this story is true, I cannot give it a fairy-tale ending. I do not know if this man returned to work and did exactly what he said he would do; his resolve may well have weakened by the time he got back home. And even if he held firm, the topsoil of midwestern farmlands has yet to be saved; the policy process is too complex to be redirected by one person's moment of truth. The man from Agriculture went on a pilgrimage into the wilderness of the human heart, and I cannot claim that his pilgrimage solved his or the topsoil's problems, any more than my pilgrimage to the Boundary Waters solves my problems or the world's.

But this I *can* claim: every time we get in touch with the truth source we carry within, there is net moral gain for all concerned. Even if we fail to follow its guidance fully, we are nudged a bit further in that direction. And the next time we are conflicted between inner truth and outer reality, it becomes harder to forget or deny that we have an inner teacher who wants to lay a claim on our lives.

As that awareness grows within us, we join in the potential for personal and social change that, in the words of Vaclav

Havel—architect of the Velvet Revolution, former president of Czechoslovakia, and seeker of political integrity—is "hidden throughout the whole of society." This potential, Havel writes, is found in "everyone who is living within the lie and who may be struck at any moment . . . by the force of truth."[4]

The divided life is a wounded life, and the soul keeps calling us to heal the wound. Ignore that call, and we find ourselves trying to numb our pain with an anesthetic of choice, be it substance abuse, overwork, consumerism, or mindless media noise. Such anesthetics are easy to come by in a society that wants to keep us divided *and* unaware of our pain—for the divided life that is pathological for individuals can serve social systems well, especially when it comes to those functions that are morally dubious.

When the man from Agriculture distances himself from his soul, it is easier for his department to report to the agribusiness lobby instead of the land. But when he, or any of us, rejoins soul and role, the institutions in which we work find it just a little bit harder to ransack another ecosystem to satisfy corporate greed or to lay off another ten thousand working poor to maximize the profits of the rich or to pass another welfare "reform" that leaves single mothers and their children worse off than they were.

Of course, if the man from Agriculture began "reporting to the land," he may well have become a less desirable employee in his superior's eyes. He may have been told to get back in line or else lose his power or even his job: institutions have been known to punish people for living integral lives.

No one wants to suffer the penalties that come from living divided no more. But there can be no greater suffering than living a lifelong lie. As we move closer to the truth that lives within us—aware that in the end what will matter most is knowing that we stayed true to ourselves—institutions start losing their sway over our lives.

This does not mean we must abandon institutions. In fact, when we live by the soul's imperatives, we gain the courage to serve institutions more faithfully, to help them resist their tendency to default on their own missions. If the man from Agriculture acted on his "farmer's heart," he did not renege on his institutional obligations but embraced them more fully, helping to call his department back to its higher purpose.

It is not easy work, rejoining soul and role. The poet Rilke—who wrote about childhood's "wingèd energy of delight" in the stanza at the start of this chapter—writes about the demands of adulthood in the final stanza of the same poem:

Take your practiced powers and stretch them out
until they span the chasm between two
contradictions. . . . For the god
wants to know himself in you.[5]

Living integral lives as adults is far more daunting than recovering our childhood capacity to commute between two worlds. As adults, we must achieve a complex integration that spans the contradictions between inner and outer reality, that supports both personal integrity and the common good. No, it is not easy work. But as Rilke suggests, by doing it, we offer what is sacred within us to the life of the world.

False Community

How does the divided self become whole? "How to do it" questions are commonplace in our pragmatic culture, and so are the mechanistic answers they often evoke: "Here is a ten-step program you can pursue in the privacy of your own home—or on the flight between JFK and LAX—to achieve an undivided life! Do these exercises, and your life will be transformed!"

Solutions of that sort are snake oil, of course. The quick-fix mentality that dominates our impatient world serves only to distract us from the lifelong journey toward wholeness. And the self-help methods so popular in our time, the best of which offer us support for that journey, sometimes reinforce the great American illusion that we can forever go it alone.

Of course, solitude is essential to personal integration: there are places in the landscapes of our lives where no one can accompany us. But because we are communal creatures who need each other's support—and because, left to our own devices, we have an endless capacity for self-absorption and self-deception—community is equally essential to rejoining soul and role.

The story of the man from Agriculture illustrates the point. Clearly, his journey had a solitary side. For weeks, he had been chewing on his problem privately, and his breakthrough came in the depths of a sleepless night, one of the most solitary times we know. But without the kind of community that surrounded him on that retreat, he might not have had his breakthrough: to avoid an endless interior recycling of his dilemma, he needed other people in whose presence he could speak his soul.

That kind of community—one that knows how to welcome the soul and help us hear its voice—I call a "circle of trust."[6]

Gathering in circles is an ancient practice being revived in our time. We have dialogue circles to improve communication, conflict resolution circles to negotiate crises, therapeutic circles to explore our emotions, problem-solving circles to puzzle out hard questions, team-building circles to cheerlead for a common cause, and collaborative learning circles to deepen our education. All of them have worthy purposes, but none of them has the singular intent of a circle of trust: to make it safe for the soul to show up and offer us its guidance.

Indeed, some circles are simply unsafe for the soul—a fact I learned the hard way as a graduate student at Berkeley in the 1960s. Like many young Americans of that era, I was learning about the inner life and hoping to bring its powers to bear on a variety of social ills. In the process, I sometimes found myself sitting in circles with people who were exploring ideas, plotting revolution, doing amateur group therapy, or brewing a mad mix of all three.

At first, these gatherings fascinated me. As one who grew up in the stoic 1950s, when we always sat in straight rows, I found Berkeley's circles exotic, energizing, and exhilarating. But my fascination soon faded. Some of those circles went round and round, taking us nowhere useful in the world. Some were thinly disguised exercises in narcissism and self-congratulatory piosity. And some were simply unsafe for human habitation: people in them were manipulated and sometimes violated by the group.

Not all circles honor the soul: some insult and invade it. I think, for example, of the so-called T-groups or encounter groups that sprang up in the 1960s. The basic ground rule for such circles is that each participant be "willing to disclose feelings that she or he may have, in the moment, about others in the group, and to solicit feedback from the others about herself or himself."[7]

Practicing that rule may evoke emotional candor. But that candor is often the kind that people come to regret as they find out how transient and untrustworthy feelings "in the moment" can be. There may be situations in which evoking instant emotion is helpful. But T-groups, even at their best, do not welcome the soul, which distrusts confrontation because its dynamics run so much deeper than momentary feelings.

Circles that scare the soul away can still be found today, not merely in the remnants of the counterculture, but at the heart of our dominant institutions. I once spoke with an executive of a Fortune 500 company that was trying to change the corporate culture. His company, he said, had been "flattening the organization" in hopes of doing its work better. The hierarchical power charts had been taken down from the office walls. Now, instead of a pyramid, there were circles in which people from the front office joined with people from the factory floor to share information, identify problems, and make decisions.

But this executive and some of his colleagues had started to understand that many people participated in those "egalitarian" circles while harboring a hierarchy within. Here is how he described the situation:

On one side of the circle sits a manager, saying silently, "OK, I'll play this game for a while. But when push comes to shove, I'm the one who has the know-how and gets paid to make this decision right. When I get back to my office, I'll find some way around whatever this group comes up with. I'll play the circle game, but I won't invest myself in it."

Meanwhile, across the circle sits a person from the shop floor, saying silently, "OK, I'll play this game for a while. But I don't get paid enough to worry about stuff like this. I just want to do my job and get back home, where I have a life, without having to take my work with me. Besides, the managers are going to figure out how to get their way with all this. I'll play the circle game, but I won't invest myself in it."

My conversation partner continued: "If we can't address these inner issues, we need to put those pyramid charts back up, because they represent what is happening in this company more honestly than our little 'circles' game. As long as we pretend to be something that we are not, our work won't get better, and it may get worse."

Even if you were not around to "do" Berkeley in the sixties and T-groups are not your style, you may have been an unwilling participant in the kind of charade I just described—it has become the standard in too many workplaces. We can put the chairs in a circle, but as long as they are occupied by people who have an inner hierarchy, the circle itself will have a divided life, one more form of "living within the lie": a false community.

✦ True Community ✦

Five years after leaving Berkeley, I found myself sitting in circles again. This time it was at Pendle Hill, a Quaker living-learning community near Philadelphia, where I spent eleven years starting in the mid-1970s. But these circles, I soon discovered, were of a different sort. They were not heady, aggressive, self-congratulatory, or manipulative. They were gentle, respectful, and reverent in the way they honored self and world, and slowly they changed my life.

In these quiet Quaker circles, people were doing neither the amateur psychotherapy nor the *faux* politics that I had experienced in Berkeley. Instead, they were doing therapy and politics rightly understood: reaching in toward their own wholeness, reaching out toward the world's needs, and trying to live their lives at the intersection of the two.

In these quiet Quaker circles, I saw people challenged, but I never saw anyone harmed. I witnessed more personal transformations than I had seen before, and I watched more people embrace their social responsibilities as well. That was when I started to understand why Quakers, who have always been few in number, have often been overrepresented in the great social issues of their time.

The circles of trust I experienced at Pendle Hill are a rare form of community—one that supports rather than supplants the individual quest for integrity—that is rooted in two basic beliefs. First, we all have an inner teacher whose guidance is more reliable than anything we can get from a doctrine, ideology, collective belief system, institution, or leader. Second, we all need other people to invite, amplify, and help us discern the inner teacher's voice for at least three reasons:

- The journey toward inner truth is too taxing to be made solo: lacking support, the solitary traveler soon becomes weary or fearful and is likely to quit the road.

- The path is too deeply hidden to be traveled without company: finding our way involves clues that are subtle and sometimes misleading, requiring the kind of discernment that can happen only in dialogue.

- The destination is too daunting to be achieved alone: we need community to find the courage to venture into the alien lands to which the inner teacher may call us.

I want to dwell for a moment on that little word *discern,* which means "distinguish between things." I think again of C. S. Lewis's tales of Narnia, that land of inwardness the children enter through the back of the magical wardrobe. There is much in Narnia that is good and beautiful, especially the voice of truth—the voice of Aslan, the great lion—that is sometimes heard in the land. But there are other voices in Narnia as well, voices of temptation, deception, darkness, and evil. It takes four children, a variety of guides, and seven volumes of pitfalls and perils to sift through this mix of messages and travel toward the truth.[8]

Occasionally, I hear people say, "The world is such a confusing place that I can find clarity only by going within." Well I, for one, find it at least as confusing "in here" as it is "out there"—usually more so!—and I think most people do. If we get lost in New York City, we can buy a map, ask a local, or find a cabbie who knows the way. The only guidance we can get on the inner journey comes through relationships in which others help us discern our leadings.

But the kind of community I learned about at Pendle Hill does not presume to do that discernment *for* us, as communities sometimes do: "You tell us your version of truth, and we will tell you whether you are right or wrong!" Instead, a circle of trust holds us in a space where we can make our own discernments, in our own way and time, in the encouraging and challenging presence of other people.

The man from Agriculture went on retreat with peers who doubtless could have offered him seasoned counsel about his dilemma. But at this moment on his journey—a moment when it was critical that he take his own soul seriously—he needed people who were willing to abstain from giving advice. He needed people who knew how to invite his soul to speak and allow him to listen.

Blessedly, the people he sat with, guided by the principles and practices that shape a circle of trust, never tried to "set him straight." Instead, they created a communal space around him where he could distinguish the inner voice of truth from the inner voice of fear. And as he spoke the truth he heard from within, these people bore witness to his self-discovery, sharpening his sense of self and strengthening his resolve to follow the inner teacher.

Here is another story about what can happen when a community welcomes the soul. In a circle I hosted, there was a good man who had been wounded by racism. In the course of our three-day retreat, he spoke only once or twice. Most of the time he sat in silence—his face, it seemed to me, a mask of sorrow. Because he was an African American in a predominantly white group, I feared not only that he was in pain but that we were in some way causing it.

For three days, I worried that this man felt like an outsider even here, in a circle that was supposed to be safe. But following the ground rules of this form of community, neither I nor anyone else tried to "fix" him. Instead, we held him and his soul in a quiet and respectful way—though it took a mighty act of will to keep from offering him consolation.

On the last morning of our retreat, I got up early. Sitting in the common room with a cup of coffee, I picked up the journal that the retreat center's staff had left there for guests to comment on their experience. On the last page, I found these words, written in a bold scrawl, signed by the man about whom I was so worried:

> Thank you for helping to deal with some of my anger. Life is too short to walk a path filled with spurs. I am not completely healed, but the process has begun. I want to give back the love and caring that was given to me. This retreat made me deal with my ghost!! Georgia/Nam/TX were all my pits. Now that the healing has started, I feel strong and for the first time capable of feeling some sense of peace.[9]

Reading those words, I realized that for the past three days, this man had been talking with his inner teacher, going much deeper in that dialogue than he could have by talking with us. Once again I felt profoundly grateful for the circles I first experienced at Pendle Hill—grateful for what they taught me about the reality and power of the soul, about a way of being together that allows the soul to make a claim on our lives, and about the miracles that can happen when we do.

If we want to renew ourselves and our world, we need more and more circles of this sort, where people who work in a large corporation can acknowledge the secret hidden in plain sight; where a conflicted farmer-turned-bureaucrat can remember that he reports to the land; where a person wounded by racism can take a step toward healing. We need more and more circles from which we can return to the world less divided and more connected to our own souls.

The circles described in this chapter ranged from ten to thirty people. But a circle of trust is not defined by numbers; it is defined by the nature of the space it creates between us. Diana Chapman Walsh, president of Wellesley College, a leader whose integrity I deeply admire, has written about the small-scale "circles" she convenes to maintain her sense of wholeness in a complex and stressful job: "I . . . come together . . . with people who bring out my better self, friends with whom I can be . . . authentic. . . . I make it a point to connect, whenever possible, with [people] with whom I have a history of shared joy and shared pain . . . who . . . call forth in me this feeling of safety."[10]

A circle of trust can form wherever two or three are gathered—as long as those two or three know how to create and protect a space for the soul.

What exactly happens in a circle of trust that supports an inner journey by making the soul feel safe? The second half of this book answers that question in considerable detail. But the practices that create a circle of trust will make little sense until we understand the two key principles behind them: that the soul or true self is real and powerful and that the soul can feel safe only in relationships that possess certain qualities. These principles are the subjects of the next two chapters.

CHAPTER III

Explorations in True Self

Intimations of the Soul

*You formed my inmost being. You knit me together
in my mother's womb. . . . I am fearfully and
wonderfully made. . . . My soul knows that very well.*

—PSALM 139:13—14

༜ Spiritual DNA ༜

When "true self" is the topic, children are the best source, because they live so close to their birthright gifts. So I begin this chapter with another reflection on childhood. But instead of revisiting my own youth, as I did in Chapter II, I want to look at someone else's early years from the vantage point of my mid-sixties.

When my first grandchild was born, I saw something in her that I had missed in my own children some twenty-five years earlier, when I was too young and self-absorbed to see anyone, including myself, very well. What I saw was clear and simple: my granddaughter arrived on earth as *this* kind of person, rather than *that*, or *that*, or *that*.

As an infant, for example, she was almost always calm and focused, quietly absorbing whatever was happening around her. She looked as if she "got" everything—enduring life's tragedies, enjoying its comedies, and patiently awaiting the day when she could comment on all of it. Today, with her verbal skills well honed, this description still fits the teenager who is one of my best friends and seems like an "old soul."

In my granddaughter I actually observed something I could once take only on faith: we are born with a seed of selfhood that contains the spiritual DNA of our uniqueness—an encoded birthright knowledge of who we are, why we are here, and how we are related to others.

We may abandon that knowledge as the years go by, but it never abandons us. I find it fascinating that the very old, who often forget a great deal, may recover vivid memories of childhood, of that time in their lives when they were most like themselves. They are brought back to their birthright nature by the abiding core of selfhood they carry within—a core made more visible, perhaps, by the way aging can strip away whatever is not truly us.

Philosophers haggle about what to call this core of our humanity, but I am no stickler for precision. Thomas Merton called it true self. Buddhists call it original nature or big self. Quakers call it the inner teacher or the inner light. Hasidic Jews call it a spark of the divine. Humanists call it identity and integrity. In popular parlance, people often call it soul. And thus far in this book, I have called it by most of these names!

What we name it matters little to me, since the origins, nature, and destiny of call-it-what-you-will are forever hidden from us, and no one can credibly claim to know its true name. But *that* we name it matters a great deal. For "it" is the objective, ontological reality of selfhood that keeps us from reducing ourselves, or each other, to biological mechanisms, psychological projections, sociological constructs, or raw material to be manufactured into whatever society needs—diminishments of our humanity that constantly threaten the quality of our lives.

"Nobody knows what the soul is," says the poet Mary Oliver; "it comes and goes / like the wind over the water."[1] But just as we can name the functions of the wind, so we can name some of the functions of the soul without presuming to penetrate its mystery:

- The soul wants to keep us rooted in the ground of our own being, resisting the tendency of other faculties, like the intellect and ego, to uproot us from who we are.

- The soul wants to keep us connected to the community in which we find life, for it understands that relationships are necessary if we are to thrive.

- The soul wants to tell us the truth about ourselves, our world, and the relation between the two, whether that truth is easy or hard to hear.

- The soul wants to give us life and wants us to pass that gift along, to become life-givers in a world that deals too much death.

All of us arrive on earth with souls in perfect form. But from the moment of birth onward, the soul or true self is assailed by deforming forces from without and within: by racism, sexism, economic injustice, and other social cancers; by jealousy, resentment, self-doubt, fear, and other demons of the inner life.

Most of us can make a long list of the external enemies of the soul, in the absence of which we are sure we would be better people! Because we so quickly blame our problems on forces "out there," we need to see how often we conspire in our own deformation: for every external power bent on twisting us out of shape, there is a potential collaborator within us. When our impulse to tell the truth is thwarted by threats of punishment, it is because we value security over being truthful. When our impulse to side with the weak is thwarted by threats of lost social standing, it is because we value popularity over being a pariah.

The powers and principalities would hold less sway over our lives if we refused to collaborate with them. But refusal is risky, so we deny our own truth, take up lives of "self-impersonation," and betray our identities.[2] And yet the soul persistently calls us back to our birthright form, back to lives that are grounded, connected, and whole.

❧ Skepticism About True Self ❧

"This is the first, wildest, and wisest thing I know," says Mary Oliver, "that the soul exists, and that it is built entirely out of attentiveness."[3] But we live in a culture that discourages us from paying attention to the soul or true self—and when we fail to pay attention, we end up living soulless lives.

Two streams in our culture contribute to our inattention. One is secularism, which regards the human self as a social construct with no created core; the other is moralism, which regards all concern for self as "selfish." Secularism and moralism may sound contradictory, but they take us to the same place: a denial of true self. If we accept their distortions of reality, the journey toward an undivided life becomes a fool's errand, so it is important to understand why both assessments of our condition are wrong.

Secularism holds that we arrive in the world not as unique individuals but as malleable raw material that receives the imprint of the gender, class, and race into which we happen to be born. We have an inherited nature, of course, a set of potentials and limits received on our roll of the genetic dice. But from a secular standpoint, it is nonsense to believe that we are born with an inviolable soul, an ontological identity, a core of created selfhood.

And yet even in the face of this cynicism, the idea of true self persists—not because of some theory but because of experiences we would not and could not have if true self were an illusion.

For example, things fall apart for someone we care about. He makes bad choices and falls into despair, and we cannot understand why. "This is not the person we know," we lament. "He is simply not himself." Or things come together for someone we care about. After years of self-alienation, she learns to love her own life. "She has come into her own," we exult. "She has finally discovered who she really is." We perceive true self in people we know and care about, and we constantly use that perception as a benchmark of their well-being.

Deeper still, we find evidence of true self in our own self-awareness, in experiences we would not have if biology, psychology, and sociology were the whole of who we are. I know I have a true self when I encounter a painful truth that my ego has tried hard to evade and am compelled by the inner teacher to confront it. I know I have a true self when my self-protective heart opens up and another person's joy or suffering fills me as if it were my own. I know I have a true self when desolation visits and I lose my taste for life and yet find within myself a life force that will not die.

But the strongest evidence for true self comes from seeing what happens when we try to live as if we did not have one, a lesson I learned on my journey with clinical depression.[4] Depressions come from a variety of causes, of course. Some result from genetic bad luck or imbalanced brain chemistry and must be treated with drugs. But others result from burying true self so deep that life becomes one long, dark night of the soul. My depression was of that kind: it responded to drugs only temporarily, returning again and again until I embraced my own truth.

The notion that depression may result from defying one's truth has received indirect support from science. Randolph Nesse, director of the Evolution and Human Adaptation Program at the University of Michigan, suggests that depression "may have developed . . . as [an evolutionary] response to situations in which a desired goal is unattainable," situations in which "one of life's paths peters out into the woods." Depression, Nesse argues, so thoroughly drains us of will and energy that we are unable to continue on a path that once seemed desirable but is—for us, at least—impassable. We must find another way, a way more suited to our nature, thus contributing to individual survival and the evolutionary success of the species.[5]

Since one of the soul's functions is to give us life and get us to pass it along—which is soul language, I suppose, for "evolutionary success"—I find it hard to distinguish here between a "biological adaptation" and an "uprising of the soul"! In fact, the metaphor Nesse chose to help explain his theory, the path that peters out into the woods, is most famously found in Dante, that master cartographer of the soul's domain: "Midway on our life's journey, I found myself / In dark woods, the right road lost."[6]

In my own case, at any rate, depression was the soul's call to stop, turn around, go back, and look for a path I could negotiate. If one ignores that call and doggedly presses on, the depression that comes from getting crosswise with true self can yield something worse than melancholy and lassitude: a deep desire to end one's life.

Such was the case with me, and looking back, I understand why. When I was living my outer life at great remove from inner truth, I was not merely on the wrong path: I was killing my selfhood with every step I took. When one's life is a walking death, the step into literal death can seem very easy to take. Medication may offer temporary relief from depressions of this sort, but the real cure goes beyond drugs. We can reclaim our lives only by choosing to live divided no more. It is a choice so daunting—or so it seems in the midst of depression—that we are unlikely to make it until our pain becomes unbearable, the pain that comes from denying or defying true self.

Secularism denies true self by regarding us as raw material. *Moralism*—the pious partner in this odd couple—achieves the same end by translating "self" into "selfishness" and insisting that we banish the word from our vocabulary. The whole problem with our society, the moralists claim, is that too many people are out for themselves at the expense of everyone else. This New Age emphasis on self-fulfillment, this constant "cult of me," is the root cause of the fragmentation of community that we see all around us. Or so the moralists argue.

Deep caring about each other's fate does seem to be on the decline, but I do not believe that New Age narcissism is much to blame. The external causes of our moral indifference are a fragmented mass society that leaves us isolated and afraid, an economic system that puts the rights of capital before the rights of people, and a political process that makes citizens into ciphers.

These are the forces that allow, even encourage, unbridled competition, social irresponsibility, and the survival of the financially fittest. The executives who brought down major corporations by taking indecent sums off the top while wage earners of modest means lost their retirement accounts were clearly more influenced by capitalist amorality than by some New Age guru.

But before I go too far in assigning blame, let me name the real problem with the moralists' complaint: there is scant evidence for their claim that the "cult of me" reigns supreme in our land. I have traveled this country extensively and have met many people. Rarely have I met people with the overweening sense of self the moralists say we have, people who put themselves first as if they possessed the divine right of kings.

Instead, I have met too many people who suffer from an empty self. They have a bottomless pit where their identity should be—an inner void they try to fill with competitive success, consumerism, sexism, racism, or anything that might give them the illusion of being better than others. We embrace attitudes and practices such as these not because we regard ourselves as superior but because we have no sense of self at all. Putting others down becomes a path to identity, a path we would not need to walk if we knew who we were.

The moralists seem to believe that we are in a vicious circle where rising individualism and the self-centeredness inherent in it cause the decline of community—and the decline of community, in turn, gives rise to more individualism and self-centeredness. The reality is quite different, I think: as community is torn apart by various political and economic forces, more and more people suffer from the empty self syndrome.

A strong community helps people develop a sense of true self, for only in community can the self exercise and fulfill its nature: giving and taking, listening and speaking, being and doing. But when community unravels and we lose touch with one another, the self atrophies and we lose touch with ourselves as well. Lacking opportunities to be ourselves in a web of relationships, our sense of self disappears, leading to behaviors that further fragment our relationships and spread the epidemic of inner emptiness.

As I view our society through the lens of my journey with depression—an extreme form of the empty self syndrome, an experience of self-annihilation just short of death—I am convinced that the moralists have got it wrong: it is never "selfish" to name, claim, and nurture true self.

There *are* selfish acts, to be sure. But those acts arise from an empty self, as we try to fill our emptiness in ways that harm others—or in ways that harm us and bring grief to those who care about us. When we are rooted in true self, we can act in ways that are life-giving for us and all whose lives we touch. Whatever we do to care for true self is, in the long run, a gift to the world.

❧ Tales of the Divided Life ❧

We arrive in this world undivided, integral, whole. But sooner or later, we erect a wall between our inner and outer lives, trying to protect what is within us or to deceive the people around us. Only when the pain of our dividedness becomes more than we can bear do most of us embark on an inner journey toward living "divided no more."

I want to examine these life passages in more detail, so I need to ask you to make (or imagine making) a simple visual aid: take a letter-sized piece of paper, cut a half-inch strip down the long side, hang on to the strip, and throw the rest away. I apologize for this cheap, low-tech device, but I am a Quaker, and this is as close as we get to a PowerPoint presentation.

Let one side of that strip represent your outer or onstage life. Here the words that describe our experience are *image, influence,* and *impact*—words that name our hopes and fears as we interact with the world. Is anyone listening to me? Am I making any difference? And how do I look while I'm trying?

Let the other side of that strip represent your inner or backstage life. Here the vocabulary is less anxious and more reflective, with words like *ideas, intuitions, feelings, values, faith*—and, deeper still, whatever words you choose to name the source from which such things come: *mind, heart, spirit, true self, soul,* or *place-beyond-all-naming.*

The relation between our backstage and onstage lives unfolds, I suggest, through four phases. Phase one comes when we arrive in this world with no separation at all between our inner and outer life. This is why most of us love to be around infants and young children: what we see is what we get. Whatever is inside an infant comes immediately to the outside, both figuratively and literally! In the presence of a newly minted human being, I am reminded of what wholeness looks like. And I am sometimes moved to wonder, "Whatever became of me?"

This phase in the relation of our onstage and backstage lives requires no visual aid: we can see it all around us in the lives of the very young. But our Quaker PowerPoint starts to become useful as we turn to phase two, that long life passage in which we build and buttress a barrier between inner truth and the outer world. So let that strip of paper—one end held in each hand, stretched out left to right at eye level, the flat surface facing you—represent the wall of separation we erect as we depart childhood en route to becoming adolescents and adults.

Some children, sadly, need this wall at home. Others do not need it until they get to school. But sooner or later, everyone needs a wall for the same reason: to protect our inward vulnerabilities against external threats. As it starts to dawn on us that the world is a dangerous place, we wall off the most fragile parts of ourselves—beliefs we hold, dimensions of our own identities—in hopes of protecting them, sometimes against great odds.

I think, for example, of the plight of many gay and lesbian young people in a society that "disapproves" of them. Stuart Mathis was a gay man who grew up in a religious community that regards homosexuality as sin. His church insisted that he "change his sexual orientation," and when he found it impossible to do so, he committed suicide, leaving these words behind:

> [My] church has no idea that as I type this letter, there are surely boys and girls on their callused knees imploring God to free them from this pain. They hate themselves. They retire to bed with their fingers pointed to their heads in the form of a gun. I am now free. I am no longer in pain and I no longer hate myself. As it turns out, God never intended for me to be straight. Perhaps my death might be a catalyst for some good.[7]

I feel nothing but compassion for people, young or old, who believe they can escape the world's cruelty only by wearing a disguise. But people sometimes wall off their truth for reasons that can only be called sinister: they conceal their identity from others because the deception provides them with a perverse form of power. The story of Saddam Hussein, ex-president of Iraq, vividly illustrates the point.

Saddam rose to power by ingratiating himself within the ranks of the then-reformist Baath Party until he had achieved enough leverage to murder the competition and consolidate his dictatorship. Hamed al-Jubouri, a former leader of the reformers, describes the capacity for dividedness that helped create Saddam's reign of terror:

> In the beginning, the Baath Party was made up of the intellectual elite of our generation. There were many professors, physicians, economists, and historians—really the nation's elite. Saddam was charming and impressive. He appeared to be totally different from what we learned he was afterward. He took all of us in. . . . We wondered about him. How could such a young man, born in the countryside north of Baghdad, become such a capable leader? He seemed both intellectual and practical. But he was hiding his real self. For years he did this, building his power quietly, charming everyone, hiding his true instincts. He has a great ability to hide his intentions; it may be his greatest skill. I remember his son Uday said one time, "My father's right shirt pocket doesn't know what is in his left shirt pocket."[8]

A case like Saddam's highlights the pathology of the divided life. But it is so large and so dramatic that it may lead us to ignore our own, less visible versions of the same disease. So let me use my journey into dividedness as a garden variety example of phase two.

I was blessed with a family where it felt safe to be myself, so my dividedness did not begin at home. But I did not feel safe at school, despite my capacity to act the role of a "successful" and "popular" student, words I put in quotation marks because the role felt so fraudulent to me. While I played my onstage part, my true self hid out backstage, fearful that the world would crush its deepest values and beliefs, its fragile hopes and yearnings.

The farther I went with my education, the less safe school became. In graduate school, especially, my emotional and spiritual survival seemed to depend on keeping my truth tucked away. When I did my doctoral work in the sociology of religion, I was, as I still am, a person of religious conviction. I did not expect my professors to share my religious beliefs or even to hold any beliefs that might be called religious. But I assumed that they would give religious phenomena the same kind of scholarly respect that historians give primary texts or geneticists give DNA or physicists give subatomic particles.

I soon learned that such was not always the case: some sociologists of religion are driven by a desire to debunk all things religious. Intimidated by professors who took this approach, I did my best during graduate school to keep my beliefs under cover—all the while, I confess, taking secret solace from W. H. Auden's witty Eleventh Commandment: "Thou shalt not . . . commit a social science."[9]

I clung to the fantasy that once I had finished my degree and could take control of my professional fate, I would no longer have to hide my truth. But I soon learned that graduate school was a picnic compared to the world of work. The deeper I moved into that world, the more need I felt to wall off my true self—trying, to put it simply, to appear smarter and tougher than I really was.

At first I needed a wall to hide my vulnerabilities from the assaults of the world. But selfhood hidden from strangers soon becomes hidden from intimates as well: the wall I reinforced to protect myself at work was not easily dismantled in the company of family and friends. I began, without even knowing it, to keep true self tucked away in my personal as well as professional life. Then—and in retrospect, inevitably—I began hiding my truth from myself as well.

Here is the ultimate irony of the divided life: live behind a wall long enough, and the true self you tried to hide from the world disappears from your own view! The wall itself and the world outside it become all that you know. Eventually, you even forget that the wall is there—and that hidden behind it is someone called "you."

Living behind a wall has at least three consequences. First, our inner light cannot illuminate the work we do in the world. When I was a young professor, walling off true self from the pressures of the tenure system meant sacrificing my teacher's heart: I lectured not to help my students learn but to prove how professorial I was. My teaching in those days was too often guided by signals from the planet called Academic Success instead of signals from within that could have kept me connected to my students' needs. I was not teaching by my best lights, and I am afraid that I too often left my students in the dark.

Second, when we live behind a wall, our inner darkness cannot be penetrated by the light that is in the world. In fact, all we can see "out there" is darkness, not realizing how much of it is of our own making! As a young man, the wall allowed me to cast my own darkness on others while remaining blissfully ignorant of how they saw me. I remember with regret the arrogance that overcame me in my thirties when I became privately judgmental of many people I knew—a posture that was, of course, no more than projected self-doubt. From time to time, courageous friends tried to shed light on my shadow, with predictable results: I judged *them* to be arrogant and refused to listen.

Third, when we live behind a wall, people close to us become wary of the gap between our onstage performance and backstage reality. Distrusting our duplicity and seeking to protect themselves, they hold us at arm's length; relationships in which we might have a chance to see ourselves more clearly disappear from our lives. As the very people who could help us see the light are repelled by the force of our shadow, we end up inhabiting a closed system, an all-embracing and self-referencing hell. Or so it was with me.

🌿 Life on the Möbius Strip 🌿

How does a closed system crack open? When the wall between soul and role blocks all external challenges that might stimulate self-knowledge, how do we even become aware that we are dangerously detached from both the world and true self?

Here, true self will come to our rescue, if we let it. The divided life is pathological, so it always gives rise to symptoms— and if we acknowledge the symptoms, we may be able to treat the disease. In my case, the symptoms became impossible to ignore. My depression returned in full force, and I was compelled to ask myself "Who am I?" not as an abstract exercise but with the urgency of real life.

Not everyone gets depressed, of course: some people start feeling aimless or anxious or angry. But at some point in phase two, having lived behind the wall for a while, most of us feel the pain of being alienated from our own truth. If we are willing to feel it and name it, instead of trying to numb it, this pain will crack our closed system open, forcing us out from behind the wall toward the healing vision of phase three.

In this phase, we reach for integration by reordering our onstage lives around our backstage values and beliefs, as can be illustrated with our Quaker PowerPoint. Take that strip of paper you were holding as a wall and join the ends together. The circle you have formed represents the yearning that drives phase three: "I want my inner truth to be the plumb line for the choices I make about my life—about the work I do and how I do it, about the relationships I enter into and how I conduct them."

This is the yearning to be "centered," a word that is, I would guess, one of the most frequently encountered in the spiritual literature of recent decades. The desire 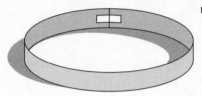 to center our outer lives on inner truth is a step toward integrity, of course. But—as our visual aid reveals in a way words alone cannot— phase three has a shadow side. Hold that ring of paper horizontally, as if it were a corral, and you will see that "getting centered" could also be described as getting the wagons in a circle or moving into a gated community or creating a secret garden where we welcome only those with whom we feel at ease.

The shadow side of phase three arises when we use inner truth as a filter to exclude anyone or anything we find challenging. Real-world examples are common: witness the divisive role religion often plays in public life, where believers on both the left and the right separate the "good guys" from the "bad guys" along doctrinal lines. When we use our truth to create such divisions, we fall far short of the open-hearted engagement with the world that all the great spiritual traditions advocate. Now the circle of phase three becomes no more than the wall of phase two in disguise.

Which brings us to the final phase in the relation of our onstage and backstage lives, where the Quaker PowerPoint becomes essential. Take that strip of paper you have been holding in the shape of a circle, pull the two ends slightly apart, give one end a half-twist, and then rejoin the two ends. You have just created a remarkable form called a Möbius strip.[10]

Holding the strip together with the fingers of one hand, use a finger on the other hand to trace what seems to be the outside surface of that strip: suddenly and seamlessly you find yourself on what seems to be the inside of the strip. Continue to trace what seems to be the inside surface of the strip: suddenly and seamlessly you find yourself on what seems to be the outside of the strip.

I have to keep repeating "what seems to be" because there is no "inside" and "outside" on the Möbius strip—the two apparent sides keep cocreating each other. The mechanics of the Möbius strip are mysterious, but its message is 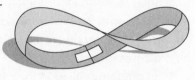 clear: whatever is inside us continually flows outward to help form, or deform, the world—and whatever is outside us continually flows inward to help form, or deform, our lives. The Möbius strip is like life itself: here, ultimately, there is only one reality.

When we understand phase four in the relation of our onstage and backstage lives, we see that phases two and three are illusions—necessary illusions, perhaps, at certain points in our lives, but illusions nonetheless. We may fool ourselves into believing that we are hiding our truth behind a wall or using our truth to screen out what is alien to us. But whether we know it or not, like it or not, accept it or not, we all live on the Möbius strip all the time: there is no place to hide! We are constantly engaged in a seamless exchange between whatever is "out there" and whatever is "in here," cocreating reality, for better or for worse.

The implications of this simple truth are widely ignored in a culture that separates inner from outer, private from public, personal from professional. When I speak to college faculty, for example, about the myth of "values-free teaching"—proposing that teachers should be open and upfront about their values—I get arguments from people who believe that it would be "unprofessional" to take their values into the classroom.

Having seen the inevitability of life on the Möbius strip, I can think of only one way to respond: "Who else are you going to send in there, then? If *you* are in the room, your *values* are in there too—and if you do not believe that, you have not been paying attention. Students are quite adept at 'psyching out' what their teachers believe. That is how students survive!" When professors—or politicians or parents—think they can mask who they are, they delude themselves and make the situation less trustworthy for others, contributing to the sense of danger that leads people to withhold self-investment.

In this fourth phase of the relation between our onstage and backstage lives, we see that we have only one choice: either we walk the Möbius strip wide awake to its continual interchanges, learning to cocreate in ways that are life-giving for ourselves and others, or we sleep-walk on the Möbius strip, unconsciously cocreating in ways that are dangerous and often death-dealing to relationships, to good work, to hope.

All of the great spiritual traditions want to awaken us to the fact that we cocreate the reality in which we live. And all of them ask two questions intended to help keep us awake: What are we sending from within ourselves out into the world, and what impact is it having "out there"? What is the world sending back at us, and what impact is it having "in here"? We are continually engaged in the evolution of self and world—and we have the power to choose, moment by moment, between that which gives life and that which deals death.

In phase four, we come full circle to the place where we began, for the Möbius strip is the adult version of the wholeness into which we were born. As T. S. Eliot famously said:

> *We shall not cease from exploration*
> *And the end of all our exploring*
> *Will be to arrive where we started*
> *And know the place for the first time.*[11]

Of course, adult wholeness is far more complex than the wholeness of infancy; it cannot be reduced to "embracing the inner child." As adults, we carry burdens and challenges children do not have—the burden of our failures, betrayals, and griefs; the challenges of our gifts, our skills, and our visions—and we must carry all of it consciously as we travel the Möbius strip.

We can survive, and even thrive, amid the complexities of adulthood by deepening our awareness of the endless inner-outer exchanges that shape us and our world and of the power we have to make choices about them. If we are to do so, we need spaces within us and between us that welcome the wisdom of the soul—which knows how to negotiate life on the Möbius strip with agility and grace. What it means to be hospitable to the soul, in solitude and in community, is the topic of the next chapter.

CHAPTER IV

Being Alone Together

A Community of Solitudes

Our disasters come from letting nothing live for itself,
from the longing we have to pull everything, even
friends, into ourselves, and let nothing alone.

—ROBERT BLY[1]

On Letting Things Alone

If we want to create spaces that are safe for the soul, we need to understand why the soul so rarely shows up in everyday life. The poet Robert Bly offers one explanation: it is our powerful ego drive "to pull everything . . . into ourselves" and let "nothing live for itself."

Behind that drive is our disbelief in the reality and power of the inner teacher. Convinced that people lack inner guidance and wishing to "help" them, we feel obliged to tell others what *we* think they need to know and how *we* think they ought to live. Countless disasters originate here—between parents and children, teachers and students, supervisors and employees—originate, that is, in presumptuous advice-giving that leaves the other feeling diminished and disrespected.

But we can learn a more creative way to be present to each other, as the following story shows. It is the story of a conflicted person who was transformed because the people around her chose to trust her inner teacher, overcoming their longtime habit of pulling everything into themselves.

It happened in a long-term circle of trust I facilitated for public school teachers. One of them, Linda, was a woman at the end of her rope. After fifteen years of teaching, she had nothing good to say about her supervisors, her colleagues, or her students—all of them, by her account, were misguided and sometimes malevolent. She felt certain that she would be a happier person and a better teacher if only she could replace all these annoying aliens with actual human beings.

The teachers who sat with Linda listened to her receptively and respectfully. Occasionally, they asked an honest, open question to help her say, and hear, more deeply what was troubling her. But guided by the ground rules of this form of community (which are explored later in this book), they offered no commentary, no argument, and no advice.

Instead, they held her in a space where Linda was compelled to listen to herself. This turned out to be a revolutionary experience for someone whose cynical view of humanity had continually been reinforced by the people to whom she complained. I do not mean the few who agreed with her. I mean those who told her she was wrong and tried to talk her out of her cynicism, as well as those who turned their backs in disgust and walked away. See, Linda would say to herself, I was right about people. No one gets it, and no one cares. Like most of us, Linda knew how to use rejection to reinforce her view of the world.

I learned how revolutionary it had been for Linda to listen to herself when she told me, after several retreats, that she intended to drop out. "It's not that I don't appreciate the group," she said. "In fact, being here has helped me understand that I don't belong in teaching anymore. The problem is not my students and colleagues; they're decent people doing the best they can. The problem is me. I've burned out on teaching, and I'm harming myself as well as others by sticking with it. I've decided to quit at the end of this year and find a different kind of job. So I guess I shouldn't be taking up space in this circle anymore."

In fact, Linda had made courageous use of her space in the circle. She had seen her shadow, stopped projecting it onto others, come to grips with her own reality, and taken a step toward wholeness. I told her she was welcome to stay.

A circle of trust, I said, has no agenda except to help people listen to their own souls and discern their own truth. Its purpose is not to help people recommit to a particular role or even become better at it, though one or both may happen. The fact that Linda had seen her shadow and now felt led to leave teaching was no less important than the vocational renewal that was happening for others in the group.

Linda stayed and continued to make good use of this community. She emerged more fully from her shadow, grieved the loss of her longtime calling, and found clues to a new vocational path that fit her gifts. She was able to listen to herself because she was with people who knew how to let her alone without abandoning her—let her be alone, that is, with her inner teacher.

ஜ Solitude and Community ஜ

As the story of Linda suggests, a circle of trust is community in a different key. *Community,* an elusive word with many shades of meaning, sometimes points to a group of people with a shared commitment to making an external impact of some sort, from changing one another to changing the world.

But a circle of trust has no such agenda. Though people's lives may be changed in such a circle—and that, in turn, may change the world a bit—the circle itself is focused on inward and invisible powers. Its singular purpose is to support the inner journey of each person in the group, to make each soul feel safe enough to show up and speak its truth, to help each person listen to his or her inner teacher.

In a circle of trust, we practice the paradox of "being alone together," of being present to one another as a "community of solitudes." Those phrases sound like contradictions because we think of solitude and community as either-or. But solitude and community, rightly understood, go together as both-and. To understand true self—which knows *who* we are in our inwardness and *whose* we are in the larger world—we need both the interior intimacy that comes with solitude and the otherness that comes with community.[2]

When we split solitude and community into an either-or and act as if we can get along with only one or the other, we put ourselves in spiritual peril. The theologian Dietrich Bonhoeffer warned us about this risk in his classic *Life Together:* "Let [the person] who cannot be alone beware of community. Let [the person] who is not in community beware of being alone."[3]

Bonhoeffer's warning is based on two simple truths. We have much to learn from within, but it is easy to get lost in the labyrinth of the inner life. We have much to learn from others, but it is easy to get lost in the confusion of the crowd. So we need solitude and community simultaneously: what we learn in one mode can check and balance what we learn in the other. Together, they make us whole, like breathing in and breathing out.

But exactly *how* solitude and community go together turns out to be trickier than breathing. When we say we are in solitude, we often bring other people with us: think of how often our "solitude" is interrupted by an interior conversation with someone who is not there! When we say we are in community, we often lose track of true self: think of how easily we can forget who we are when we get entangled in group dynamics.

If we are to hold solitude and community together as a true paradox, we need to deepen our understanding of both poles. *Solitude* does not necessarily mean living apart from others; rather, it means never living apart from one's self. It is not about the absence of other people—it is about being fully present to ourselves, whether or not we are with others. *Community* does not necessarily mean living face-to-face with others; rather, it means never losing the awareness that we are connected to each other. It is not about the presence of other people—it is about being fully open to the reality of relationship, whether or not we are alone.

When we understand solitude and community in these ways, we also understand what it means to create a circle of trust—a space between us that is hospitable to the soul, a community of solitudes where we can be alone together.

If the idea of "creating a space between us" sounds exotic or bizarre, consider the fact that we do it all the time. Whenever people come together, in numbers large or small, we create different kinds of spaces to support different purposes:

- We know how to create spaces that invite the *intellect* to show up, analyzing reality, parsing logic and arguing its case: such spaces can be found, for example, in universities.

- We know how to create spaces that invite the *emotions* into play, reacting to injury, expressing anger and celebrating joy: they can be found in therapy groups.

- We know how to create spaces that invite the *will* to emerge, consolidating energy and effort on behalf of a shared goal: they can be found in task forces and committees.

- We certainly know how to create spaces that invite the *ego* to put in an appearance, polishing its image, protecting its turf and demanding its rights: they can be found wherever we go!

- But we know very little about creating spaces that invite the *soul* to make itself known. Apart from the natural world, such spaces are hard to find—and we seem to place little value on preserving the soul spaces in nature.

I am not suggesting that the intellect, emotions, will, and ego are irrelevant to inner work. Operating independently, these faculties will not take us where the soul wants to go. But they are all vital parts of being human, and—with guidance from the soul—they can all become vital allies on the journey toward an undivided life.

When the soul speaks through the intellect, we learn to think "with the mind descended into the heart."[4] When it speaks through the emotions, our feelings are more likely to nurture relationships. When it speaks through the will, our willpower can be harnessed for the common good. When it speaks through the ego, we gain a sense of self that gives us the courage to speak truth to power. Every human faculty, as it becomes more soulful, can help us negotiate the complex terrain of life on the Möbius strip.

𝕰 The Soul Is Shy 𝕰

Spaces designed to welcome the soul and support the inner journey are rare. But the principles and practices that shape such spaces are neither new nor untested.

Some are embedded in monastic tradition, for the monastery is the archetypal "community of solitudes." Some emerged over four hundred years of Quaker faith and practice. Some were revived in the transpersonal psychology movement of the mid-twentieth century. And some are embodied in the processes of spiritual formation that can be found at the heart of most of the world's great wisdom traditions.

Formation may be the best name for what happens in a circle of trust, because the word refers, historically, to soul work done in community. But a quick disclaimer is in order, since *formation* sometimes means a process quite contrary to the one described in this book—a process in which the pressure of orthodox doctrine, sacred text, and institutional authority is applied to the misshapen soul in order to conform it to the shape dictated by some theology. This approach is rooted in the idea that we are born with souls deformed by sin, and our situation is hopeless until the authorities "form" us properly.

But all of that is turned upside down by the principles of a circle of trust: I applaud the theologian who said that "the idea of humans being born alienated from the Creator would seem an abominable concept."[5] Here formation flows from the belief that we are born with souls in perfect form. As time goes on, we are subject to powers of deformation, from within as well as without, that twist us into shapes alien to the shape of the soul. But the soul never loses its original form and never stops calling us back to our birthright integrity.

In a circle of trust, the powers of deformation are held at bay long enough for the soul to emerge and speak its truth. Here we are not required to conform ourselves to some external template. Instead, we are invited to conform our lives to the shape of our own souls. In a circle of trust, we can grow our selfhood like a plant—from the potential within the seed of the soul, in ground made fertile by the quality of our relationships, toward the light of our own wholeness—trusting the soul to know its own shape better than any external authority possibly can.

What sort of space gives us the best chance to hear soul truth and follow it? A space defined by principles and practices that honor the soul's nature and needs. What is that nature, and what are those needs? My answer draws on the only metaphor I know that reflects the soul's essence while honoring its mystery: the soul is like a wild animal.

Like a wild animal, the soul is tough, resilient, resourceful, savvy, and self-sufficient: it knows how to survive in hard places. I learned about these qualities during my bouts with depression. In that deadly darkness, the faculties I had always depended on collapsed. My intellect was useless; my emotions were dead; my will was impotent; my ego was shattered. But from time to time, deep in the thickets of my inner wilderness, I could sense the presence of something that knew how to stay alive even when the rest of me wanted to die. That something was my tough and tenacious soul.

Yet despite its toughness, the soul is also shy. Just like a wild animal, it seeks safety in the dense underbrush, especially when other people are around. If we want to see a wild animal, we know that the last thing we should do is go crashing through the woods yelling for it to come out. But if we will walk quietly into the woods, sit patiently at the base of a tree, breathe with the earth, and fade into our surroundings, the wild creature we seek might put in an appearance. We may see it only briefly and only out of the corner of an eye—but the sight is a gift we will always treasure as an end in itself.

Unfortunately, *community* in our culture too often means a group of people who go crashing through the woods together, scaring the soul away. In spaces ranging from congregations to classrooms, we preach and teach, assert and argue, claim and proclaim, admonish and advise, and generally behave in ways that drive everything original and wild into hiding. Under these conditions, the intellect, emotions, will, and ego may emerge, but not the soul: we scare off all the soulful things, like respectful relationships, goodwill, and hope.

A circle of trust is a group of people who know how to sit quietly "in the woods" with each other and wait for the shy soul to show up. The relationships in such a group are not pushy but patient; they are not confrontational but compassionate; they are filled not with expectations and demands but with abiding faith in the reality of the inner teacher and in each person's capacity to learn from it. The poet Rumi captures the essence of this way of being together: "A circle of lovely, quiet people / becomes the ring on my finger."[6]

Few of us have experienced large-scale communities that possess these qualities, but we may have had one-on-one relationships that do. By reflecting on the dynamics of these small-scale circles of trust, we can sharpen our sense of what a larger community of solitudes might look like—and remind ourselves that two people who create safe space for the soul can support each other's inner journey.

Think, for example, about someone who helped you grow toward true self. When I think about such a person, it is my father who first comes to mind. Though he was himself a hardworking and successful businessman, he did not press me toward goals that were his rather than mine. Instead, he made space for me to grow into my own selfhood. Throughout high school, I got mediocre grades—every one of which I earned—although I always did quite well on standardized intelligence tests. I look back with amazement on the fact that not once did my father demand that I "live up to my potential." He trusted that if I had a gift for academic life, it would flower in its own time, as it did when I went to college.

The people who help us grow toward true self offer unconditional love, neither judging us to be deficient nor trying to force us to change but accepting us exactly as we are. And yet this unconditional love does not lead us to rest on our laurels. Instead, it surrounds us with a charged force field that makes us want to grow from the inside out—a force field that is safe enough to take the risks and endure the failures that growth requires.

That is not only what my father did for me; it is an element in every such story I have ever heard. We grow toward true self in a space where our growth is not driven by external demands but drawn forward, by love, into our own best possibilities.

Here is one way to understand the relationships in a circle of trust: they combine unconditional love, or regard, with hopeful expectancy, creating a space that both safeguards and encourages the inner journey. In such a space, we are freed to hear our own truth, touch what brings us joy, become self-critical about our faults, and take risky steps toward change—knowing that we will be accepted no matter what the outcome.

There is another one-on-one relationship that reveals, in microcosm, how we are called to relate to each other in a circle of trust. I am thinking of the experience some of us have had at the bedside of a dying person, "accompanying" someone who is making the most solitary journey of all.

When we sit with a dying person, we gain two critical insights into what it means to "be alone together." First, we realize that we must abandon the arrogance that often distorts our relationships—the arrogance of believing that we have the answer to the other person's problem. When we sit with a dying person, we understand that what is before us is not a "problem to be solved" but a mystery to be honored. As we find a way to stand respectfully on the edge of that mystery, we start to see that all of our relationships would be deepened if we could play the fixer role less frequently.

Second, when we sit with a dying person, we realize that we must overcome the fear that often distorts our relationships—the fear that causes us to turn away when the other reveals something too vexing, painful, or ugly to bear. Death may be all of this and more. And yet we hold the dying person in our gaze, our hearts, our prayers, knowing that it would be disrespectful to avert our eyes, that the only gift we have to offer in this moment is our undivided attention.

When people sit with a dying person, they know that they are doing more than taking up space in the room. But if you ask them to describe what that "more" is, they have a hard time finding the right words. And when the words come, they are almost always some variant on "I was simply being present."

We learn to "practice presence" when we sit with a dying person—to treat the space between us as sacred, to honor the soul and its destiny. Our honoring may be wordless or perhaps mediated by speech that the dying person cannot hear. Yet this honoring somehow keeps us connected as we bear witness to another's journey into the ultimate solitude.

I am not privy to reports from the other side, so I do not know what having someone "practicing presence" means to a person who is dying. But I have a hunch that comes from my own experience. When I went into a deadly darkness that I had to walk alone, the darkness called clinical depression, I took comfort and strength from those few people who neither fled from me nor tried to save me but were simply present to me. Their willingness to be present revealed *their* faith that I had the inner resources to make this treacherous trek—quietly bolstering *my* faltering faith that perhaps, in fact, I did.

I do not know, yet, what a dying person experiences. But this I do know: I would sooner die in the company of someone practicing simple presence than I would die alone. And I know this as well: we are all dying, all the time. So why wait for the last few hours before offering each other our presence? It is a gift we can give and receive right now, in a circle of trust.

✿⥱ Two Solitudes ⥲✿

No one has described the relationships that characterize a circle of trust more beautifully or more precisely than the poet Rainer Maria Rilke, who wrote of "the love that consists in this, that two solitudes protect and border and salute each other."[7]

A love of this sort makes the soul feel safe, for at least two reasons. First, it excludes the violence we sometimes do to each other in love's name. I do not mean the overt, physical violence of an abusive relationship. I mean the subtle violence we do when we violate the other's solitude with the intention of being helpful.

In *Zorba the Greek*, Nikos Kazantzakis tells a tale about the way some efforts to help can do real harm:

> One morning . . . I discovered a cocoon in the bark of a tree, just as the butterfly was making a hole in the case preparing to come out. I waited a while, but it was too long appearing and I was impatient. I bent over it and breathed on it to warm it. I warmed it as quickly as I could and the miracle

began to happen before my eyes, faster than life. The case opened, the butterfly started slowly crawling out and I shall never forget my horror when I saw how its wings were folded back and crumpled; the wretched butterfly tried with its whole body to unfold them. Bending over it I tried to help it with my breath. In vain.

It needed to be hatched out patiently and the unfolding of the wings should be a gradual process in the sun. Now it was too late. My breath had forced the butterfly to appear all crumpled, before its time. It struggled desperately and, a few seconds later, died in the palm of my hand.

That little body is, I do believe, the greatest weight I have on my conscience. For I realize today that it is a mortal sin to violate the great laws of nature. We should not hurry, we should not be impatient, but we should confidently obey the eternal rhythm.[8]

On rare occasions, we may need to breathe someone into life who is incapacitated in a way that threatens his or her well-being. But most people can and must come to life in their own way and time, and if we try to help them by hastening the process, we end up doing harm. In a circle of trust—as two or more solitudes protect and border and salute each other—we are given the freedom to live our own lives by "the great laws of nature" and to learn how to live them more deeply.

There is a sharper way to put this point: a love that respects the other's solitude offers a hedge against amateur psychotherapy, an abomination that has created many "circles of distrust." A circle of trust is not a therapy group. It is not facilitated by a professional therapist, and its members do not have a therapeutic contract with each other. In an age when therapy is practiced without credentials, competence, or invitation, the image of two solitudes protecting, bordering, and saluting each other can help

keep us from falling into this common form of interpersonal violence.

The second reason this sort of love makes the soul feel safe is
the hedge it provides against benign neglect. When we understand
that our efforts to help other people can be unhelpful, or worse,
we may start to avert our eyes from their struggles and pains, not
knowing what to do and embarrassed by our own ineptitude. If
our efforts to "fix" others do not help them, and might even harm
them, what is left except to walk away?

Rilke's image of love offers us a third possibility. Instead of
fixing up, or letting down, people who have a problem, we stand
with simple attentiveness at the borders of their solitude—trusting
that they have within themselves whatever resources they need
and that our attentiveness can help bring those resources into play.

*A circle of trust consists of relationships that are neither invasive
nor evasive.* In this space, we neither invade the mystery of another's
true self nor evade another's struggles. We stay present to each other
without wavering, while stifling any impulse to fix each other up.
We offer each other support in going where each needs to go, and
learning what each needs to learn, at each one's pace and depth.

There is one more way to describe the love that creates a circle of trust: it is a love that requires us to treat the soul as an end in
itself. We often relate to each other as means to our own ends,
extending "respect" to each other in hopes of getting something for
ourselves. Under those conditions, certain faculties, such as the
ego, will show up to see if there is something to be gained.

But the soul will show up only if we approach each other
with no other motive than the desire to welcome it. When we
"protect and border and salute" each other's solitude, we break our
manipulative habits and make it safe for the soul to emerge.

I think again of the man from the Department of Agriculture. If the people on that retreat had tried to use him to get leverage on public policy, I do not think he could have heard his soul

say, "You report to the land." Treated as a means to other people's political ends, he would have responded from his intellect, emotions, will, or ego, but his soul would have been in full retreat. He was able to hear his soul speak in a way that had political consequences only because nobody tried to use his soul to that end.

There is a challenging paradox here, and it is key to circles of trust. Honoring the soul will have outcomes for our work in the world. But if we want those outcomes to occur, we must approach the soul for no reason other than to honor it, making no effort to direct or demand certain outcomes.

It is a paradox best explained with a story. I was once visited by the leaders of a community whose schools were being torn by racial and ethnic tensions; they wanted my help in creating circles of trust to alleviate this crisis. As much as I cared about their plight, I had to tell them I could not help—at least, not under these circumstances—because their request reflected a misconception of what makes a circle trustworthy to the soul.

You cannot gather people and say, in effect, "In this circle, we invite your soul to speak so we can resolve our racial tensions." The moment you do so, an impossible distortion sets in: I am in the circle because I have a "white soul," he is here because he has an "African American soul," and she is here because she has a "Hispanic soul." But the soul has no race or ethnicity: it is the core of our shared humanity as well as our individual uniqueness. The moment we try to trap it in sociological categories, hoping to get leverage on some problem, it will run away as fast as it can because we have distorted its nature.

When we create a space where the soul feels safe, it will help us deal with our most divisive issues: I have seen it happen many times around race, class, sexual orientation, and other contentious matters. And yet to invite the soul to show up in order to solve a social problem is to scare it away as surely as when we set out to fix another person.

In our utilitarian culture, it is hard to hold fast to the notion that a circle of trust is not about solving a visible problem: it is about honoring an invisible thing called the soul. But when we learn to trust the invisible powers within us, we will watch ourselves, other people, our institutions, and our society grow in integrity.

What We Trust

What exactly do we trust in a circle of trust? Four things, at least:

- We trust the soul, its reality and power, its self-sufficiency, its capacity to speak truth, its ability to help us to listen and respond to what we hear.

- We trust each other to have the intention, discipline, and goodwill to create and hold a space that is safe enough to welcome the soul.

- We trust the principles and practices that create such a space and safeguard the relationships within it, aware that the pull of conventional culture is persistent and can easily tug us toward behaviors that will scare the shy soul away.

- We trust that welcoming the soul with no "change agenda" in mind can have transforming outcomes for individuals and institutions.

In the chapters to come, I describe in some detail the practices required to create a circle of trust. But before I end this chapter, I want to tell a real-life story that shows what it is like, in practice, to trust the soul, each other, the principles and practices, and the claim that transformation may occur precisely because we do not demand it.[9]

In a long-term group I facilitated for public school educators, there was a veteran high school shop teacher who, by his own admission, did not "get it." Through the first six of eight retreats, Tim sat in silence, looking uncomfortable, distracted, and sometimes disdainful of the process. And in each of those six retreats, he took me aside to ask, "What the hell is going on in there?" Six times I told him that his question, though heartfelt, was not one I could answer for him.

As the seventh retreat got under way, it quickly became clear that something had happened to Tim, and he was eager to tell us about it. For the past two years, he said, he had been locked in a power struggle with his principal, who had insisted that he attend a summer institute on the new, high-tech method of teaching shop. For two years, Tim had responded to his principal with an equally insistent and increasingly angry "No!"

"This high-tech stuff," he told his principal, "is just another fad that will fade away. And even if it doesn't, it's not what my students need right now. They need hands-on experience! I should know. I've been teaching shop for twenty years. That summer institute is a crock, and I'm not going to waste my time or your money attending it."

For two years, Tim and his principal had been in the ring with each other, and a few weeks earlier, the bell had rung for round three. Once again the principal called Tim in and made his demand, and once again Tim refused.

But this time, Tim said something new. "For the past year and a half," he told his principal, "I've been sitting with this group of teachers who've been exploring their inner lives—and I've begun to realize that I have one, too! I can see now that I've been lying to myself, and to you, about why I won't go to the summer institute.

"The truth is, I'm afraid. I'm afraid I won't understand what they are saying. I'm afraid that what I *do* understand will make me feel like I've been teaching the wrong way for twenty years. I'm afraid I'll come home from that institute feeling like I'm over the hill. I still don't want to go, but at least I can be honest with you about why."

Tim paused for a moment and then continued. "My principal and I sat there in silence for a while, staring at the floor. Then he looked up at me and said, 'You know what? I'm afraid, too. Let's go together.'"

That story embodies much of what I want to say about the power of a circle of trust. It reveals what can happen when a person is given space to listen to his or her soul, hear its voice, and find the courage to act on what it says. It reveals the power of truth-telling to transform us, our relationships, and our work in the world. As Tim later said of himself, after he and his principal had returned from the summer institute, "I'm no longer in despair. My vocation as a teacher has been renewed."

But this story is not only about Tim, a teacher transformed. It is also about a circle of people who allowed Tim to take an inner journey at his own pace and in his own way, trusting that the truth he needed was available from within and would come to him when he was ready for it. They did not try to force the butterfly into life, nor did they walk away not caring if it died. In this circle of trust, Tim was neither invaded nor evaded, and that allowed him to arrive at a life-changing insight he might never have reached otherwise.

During those first six retreats, anyone who had taken Psychology 101 could have sized Tim up with ease, so transparent was his condition: "You know what? Your problem is that you're afraid." But if people had approached him that way, he would have done what we all do when we are invaded: he would have resisted the diagnosis with all his might while his soul truth receded deeper into the woods.

During those first six retreats, the group could easily have turned on Tim, as groups often do, shunning or judging someone because they are threatened by the person's behavior: "Come on! Get with the program! Stop sending all those nonverbal messages that make the rest of us feel like fools. Participate, or give up your seat to someone who will!"

But nothing like that happened. Guided by the principles and practices of a circle of trust, no one tried to analyze Tim or set him straight. No one responded to his behavior as a judgment on themselves or the group. No one judged him in order to assuage their own feelings. Instead, everyone held Tim in an open, trusting, and trustworthy space, neither taking nor giving offense, until he learned what he needed to learn from his own inner teacher— a lesson made possible by a community that knew how to "protect and border and salute" Tim's solitude.

What is required to create and protect such a space? That question is the focus of the next five chapters.

CHAPTER V

Preparing for the Journey

Creating Circles of Trust

*I pin my hopes to quiet processes and small circles, in
which vital and transforming events take place.*
—RUFUS JONES[1]

ᕕ Catch-22 ᕗ

Catch-22, Joseph Heller's classic novel on the lunacy of war, parsed the "logic" that governs a bomber pilot's life. If you understand the danger you are in and ask to be relieved of your duties, you cannot be granted relief. Why? Because the fact that you understand the danger means that you are sane, and only pilots who are crazy can be relieved of their duties. So you must keep flying even though you are crazy to do so! Catch-22 has proven to be an apt image for our time, which seems full of "problematic situations whose only solution is denied by circumstances inherent in the problem."[2]

I am often reminded of catch-22 when I talk with people about joining or forming a circle of trust. People who feel at risk of losing touch with their souls will say that they need such a circle. Yet they often claim that their fragmented and frenzied lives—the lives that put them at risk—make it impossible for them to join! The very situation that creates our need for safe space seems to prevent us from getting what we need.

But hidden in that little phrase "seems to" is the way out of catch-22. The notion that we cannot have what we genuinely need is a culturally induced illusion that keeps us mired in the madness of business as usual. But illusions are made to be broken. Am I busy? Of course I am. Am I too busy to live my own life? Only if I value it so little that I am willing to surrender it to the enemy.

We cannot get snared in catch-22 unless we consent to it, so the way out is clear: we must become conscientious objectors to the forces that put us at war with ourselves, assaulting our identity and integrity, violating the sanctity of our souls.

I am no stranger to the difficulty of taking such a stand, but participating in circles of trust has helped me find the courage to do so. In the process, I have learned that belonging to such circles not only fits within the confines of our busy lives but can also help free us from those confines. So with a salute to all who have defied catch-22—and in the service of all who intend to—I want to explore five features of this form of community that make it accessible, attractive, and generative, even in the midst of much madness: clear limits, skilled leadership, open invitations, common ground, and graceful ambiance.

Clear Limits

No matter how much we may feel the need for a circle of trust, few of us can imagine taking time for community "on top of everything else." And even if we can, we find it hard to imagine that other people would be able or willing to come along with us.

But our dilemma is only partly due to the number of hours in a day. It is also due to the fact that *community*—a kaleidoscopic word that assumes new meanings at every turn—can evoke utopian images of a bygone era, a slower, simpler time when people lived side by side in villages and small towns. If community is to become an option for more than a fortunate few, we must shake off these romantic fantasies and create forms of life together that respect contemporary realities.

Circles of trust do exactly that because they have boundaries that traditional communities lack. Such circles, for example, do not depend on a critical mass of people the way a traditional community does; two people who know how to "protect and border and salute" each other's solitude can form a circle of trust. Of course, our opportunities for mutual illumination increase as the size of the circle grows, with about twenty-five people as the outside limit. But a couple, or a small group, who create safe space for the soul, can support each other on the journey toward an undivided life.

Unlike a traditional community, a circle of trust need not be the constant context of our lives. It can be a group of people with whom we meet once a week for an hour or two, once a month for the better part of a day, or three times a year for a weekend. And our commitment to each other should have an end point, agreed on in advance—say, twelve months from the first gathering. With this proviso, people can depart gracefully if the experience is not supportive or renew their participation if it is.

Unlike a traditional community, a circle of trust need not be limited to people who live nearby. One of the most important circles in my life involves people from around the country who gather only two or three times a year. But we share such a strong culture of soul-honoring relationships that we pick up like old friends every time we meet, as if we had never been apart.

Unlike a traditional community, a circle of trust need not be the singular matrix of our lives; we invariably belong to communities of other sorts. And unlike a traditional community, a circle of trust need not be freestanding but can be embedded in a setting that has an ongoing institutional life, such as a religious congregation or a workplace.

A circle of trust may lack size, scope, and continuity as compared to a traditional community. But it makes up for what it lacks by being intentional about its life—about why we are together, about where we want to go, and about how we must relate to each other if we are to reach our destination.

Other forms of community often lack this intentionality, weakening their impact on people's lives. Churches, for example, ask members to affirm certain religious beliefs and the mission those beliefs imply. But rarely are churches intentional about naming—let alone asking members to commit themselves to—the relational norms and practices that would support their beliefs and mission. As a result, the relationships within many churches are shaped more by the norms of secular culture than by those of the religious tradition.

For example, many congregations proclaim the belief that salvation comes from grace alone. But because they have no relational practices grounded in this principle, members often persist in the cultural habit of trying to "save" each other, contradicting their own theology and driving each other's souls into hiding. That is why I sometimes hear churchgoers say that they cannot take their most painful problems into the heart of the church community, where relationships tend to be invasive.

Yet in a circle of trust, I often hear participants say, "What goes on here is what I had hoped my religious community would be like." A small circle of limited duration that is intentional about its process will have a deeper, more life-giving impact than a large, ongoing community that is shaped by the norms of conventional culture.

The intentionality of a circle of trust can even transform the cramped sense of time that keeps us from taking community seriously. Belonging to such a circle takes time. But when the hours we spend together have meaningful outcomes for our lives, time stops feeling scarce. Time, and life itself, becomes more abundant as we learn to live more responsively to the wisdom of the soul.

✿ Skilled Leadership ✿

A second condition for a circle of trust is a skilled leader, or facilitator, who is well grounded in the principles and practices necessary to create safe space for the soul.

Of course, two people who know how to "protect and border and salute" each other's solitude do not need a third to facilitate. With thoughtful preparation, they can hold such a space by and for themselves. In fact, every circle of trust, regardless of size, requires that everyone in it help hold safe space: witness the story of the shop teacher who confronted his own fear because no one in his circle invaded or evaded him.

But the larger the circle, the more important it is to have a designated leader. The norms of a circle of trust are profoundly countercultural: "Thou shalt not even *try* to save each other!" But the gravitational field of conventional culture constantly tugs us toward invasive ways of relating: "Saving each other is why we were put here on earth!" The larger the circle, the more likely it is that someone will succumb to gravity, so we need a leader who can arrest the free fall and make the space safe again.

Unfortunately, our idea of leadership has been deformed by a myth that links leadership to hierarchy, as if leaders were needed only in systems that operate from the top down. But when we are in "community"—which, at a turn of the kaleidoscope, evokes the romance of an instinctive life together—we can dispense with a designated leader, allowing the role to pass spontaneously from one person to the next. Or so goes the myth.

Yet in my experience, a community requires more leadership than a hierarchy does. A hierarchy has clear goals, a well-established division of labor, and a set of policies about how things are supposed to run; if the machine is well designed and well lubricated, it can almost run itself. A community is a chaotic, emergent, and creative force field that needs constant tending. And when a community's aims are countercultural, as they are in a circle of trust, its need for tending is even greater. Lacking a leader grounded in the principles, skilled at the practices, and granted the authority to lead, a circle of trust will fail because the relational culture it requires is so rare and so fragile.

The authority such a leader needs is not the same as power. Power comes to anyone who controls the tools of coercion, which range from grades to guns. But authority comes only to those who are granted it by others. And what leads us to grant someone authority? The word itself contains a clue: we grant authority to people we perceive as "authoring" their own words and actions, people who do not speak from a script or behave in prepro-grammed ways.

In other words, we grant authority to people we perceive as living undivided lives. Since the purpose of a circle of trust is to help us live that way, the leader, or facilitator, must also be a par-ticipant in the circle: standing apart from the process, as leaders sometimes do, becomes a sign of dividedness that undermines one's authority with the group.

The role of facilitator-participant is both demanding and rewarding. Being personally invested in the process helps my own journey along and gives the group confidence in my legitimacy as a leader. But I cannot let my needs take up space that I should be protecting for others, let alone make others feel that I am too frag-ile to lead. As facilitator-participant, I must maintain a balance, participating in ways that "authorize" me to lead but not in ways that might weaken my authority.

The facilitator's role in a circle of trust is easily defined: to be first among equals in creating and protecting a space where every-one's soul can feel safe. But that role is not so easily played. It requires grounding, training, mentoring, and experience. Deeper still, a facilitator must understand the solemn responsibility that accompanies a work in which people are invited to make their souls vulnerable and promised that they will be done no harm.

This book is my best effort at explaining the principles and practices that make for good facilitation of a circle of trust. But such leadership requires experience that no book can provide, so there is a note at the back of this book with information about a face-to-face facilitator preparation program.[3]

There may be people who are already qualified to facilitate a circle of trust by virtue of personal gifts and past experience. But most people who do this work will say what I say: holding a space for the soul is more challenging than any other kind of leadership I have attempted, and I needed mentoring to do it wisely and well.

❧ Open Invitations ❧

A third condition for a circle of trust is that everyone's participation in it be a voluntary response to an open invitation, without a hint of the manipulation or coercion that would scare off the shy soul.

Employers, for example, cannot require employees to join a circle of trust—a point so obvious I would not mention it had I not observed a tendency in this direction under the guise of "community-building" or "spirituality" in the workplace. Employers can and should create sanction-free spaces where employees may do some truth-telling for the sake of personal and corporate health. Yet—as the story of that large corporation with its "hierarchical circles" reveals—nothing makes the soul flee faster than being told it must sing for its supper!

But the coercion that undermines circles of trust goes well beyond an employer who demands that employees "bare their souls." People often join a group voluntarily and *then* experience pressures to conform. These pressures may be so subtle that our egos barely register them, but that seismograph called the soul is quick to feel the shocks. If we want to welcome the soul, we must avoid pressure of any sort.

I can illustrate what I mean—and say a bit more about the art of facilitation—by describing the opening moments in a newly formed circle of trust. To establish the norms of this new counterculture, I begin by reassuring the people that

> this is not a "share or die" event! As this retreat proceeds, I
> will issue invitations, not orders. If I ever extend an invita-

tion you don't want to accept, please do whatever you need to do—and do it knowing that you have the full support of the group, no questions asked. For example, if I invite folks into small groups, and you need time alone, feel free to take it. If you want to be in a small group but don't want to answer the question I have posed, make up your own question and answer it. Your soul knows better than I what you need to do.

Having offered people freedom of choice, I need to "walk my talk" with every step I take, or the space becomes unsafe and I lose my authority to lead. But this turns out to be trickier than it may seem. Take, for example, the simple matter of inviting people to introduce themselves during the opening session: "I invite you to tell us your name and, if you wish, say a few words about something that makes you feel fully alive."

Most people will want to say something about themselves, in part because the question I have posed, and the way I framed it, leave them free to respond at whatever level of vulnerability they choose. But one or two people may wish to remain silent—and if I do anything that makes them feel compelled to speak, I become untrustworthy for them and perhaps for others.

So I do not structure self-introductions by saying, "I'll introduce myself first; then let's go around the circle to my right." Doing so would create a forced march that deprives people of their freedom. Instead, I say, "Let's begin with some silence. When someone is ready to introduce himself or herself, that person is invited to do so, followed by whoever wants to go next, until the last person who wants to speak has done so."

Once in a while, as the self-introductions come toward an end, I am aware that there is someone who has not yet spoken. I do not know whether or not this person wants to speak. But if I ask directly, or even cast a questioning glance in his or her direction, I have betrayed the principle of noncoercion. I have thrown the spotlight on someone who may have decided not to speak and have implied that I would prefer it if he or she would decide otherwise! Now I have lost the trust of at least one person who sees that the soul's freedom ends where my agenda begins.

At such a moment, my task as a facilitator is to hold the space for a while, with my eyes closed or cast down to the center of the circle. Then, without looking at anyone, I can say: "Let's take another minute or two in silence to make sure that everyone who wants to speak has had a chance. Then we will take a next step."

Now I have honored my promise to give everyone a free choice while still making sure that no one gets cut off. On several occasions, people have come to me later, saying, "I was not ready to speak during our opening circle. Thank you for not forcing me to do so—you helped me trust the process. But I would like to introduce myself when the group comes back together."

When a facilitator holds the space this way, he or she sends a reassuring message to all concerned: "I meant it when I said that this is not a 'share or die' event. I am here not only to name the norms for this circle but also to model what it means to live by them. I will do what I can to keep this space safe for your soul." Sending that message clearly and consistently is key to safeguarding a circle of trust.

✌ Common Ground ✌

A fourth condition for a circle of trust is the creation of common ground on which people of diverse beliefs can explore issues of the inner life. Common ground is especially critical in secular settings, such as public schools, where pluralism must be honored. It may even be important in settings such as churches where we assume that people share certain beliefs. In a circle of trust—where people feel free to speak in their own words about what they really believe—they sometimes turn out to have less in common than we, or they, thought.

But as we create open ground that welcomes diversity, we cannot allow people to wander aimlessly. The soul wants hospitality, but it also wants honesty, wants to engage challenging questions that we would prefer to avoid. How can we keep the circle open to diverse views while keeping it focused on difficult truths? If we cannot answer that question, our conversations will not take us to the depths, and the truth-loving soul will leave the room.

In certain long-term circles of trust, we create common ground that is both open and focused by framing our exploration in the metaphors of the seasons.[4] Time after time, these metaphors have proved their capacity to host a respectful discourse, focused on challenging questions, among diverse voices. Seasonal metaphors help people speak about issues we often evade, in whatever language has meaning for the speaker, without anyone giving or taking offense.

I can illustrate with a sample metaphor for each of the four seasons. We often start our groups in the fall, a time when work begins again for many people, following a summer break—and nature begins her work again by dropping and scattering seeds. In this season of new beginnings, a circle of trust might inquire into the "seed of true self."

What seed was planted when you or I arrived on earth with our identities intact? How can we recall and reclaim those birthright gifts and potentials? We explore these questions through autobiography, sharing childhood stories that contain clues about who we were before forces within and around us began to deform our sense of true self. Through such storytelling, I have seen burned-out teachers reclaim the passion that took them into teaching and resolve not to let anyone rob them of it again.

But the seeds of possibility planted with such hope in the fall must eventually endure winter, when the potentials we carried at birth appear to be dead and gone. As we look out upon the winter landscape of our lives, it seems clear that whatever was seeded in the fall is now buried deep in the snow, frozen over and winter-killed. Many demoralized people recognize this "dead of winter" metaphor as an all-too-apt description of their bleak inner lives.

Yet when we understand winter in the natural world, we realize that what we see out there is not death so much as dormancy. Some life has died, of course. But much of it has gone underground, into hibernation, awaiting a season of renewal and rebirth. So winter invites us to name whatever feels dead in us, to wonder whether it might in fact be dormant—and to ask how we can help it, and ourselves, "winter through."

It can be a powerful experience to realize how much dormancy we contain. As adults, we like to pretend that we are complete. If we are willing to drop that pretense and acknowledge all that remains unrealized in our lives, good things may happen, and not just for us. When teachers discover what is dormant in themselves, for example, they become more perceptive about what is dormant in their students—and become better teachers as a result. People who have had a great teacher almost always say, "That teacher saw something in me that I was unable to see in myself."

Spring is the season of surprise when we realize once again that despite our perennial doubts, winter's darkness yields to light and winter's deaths give rise to new life. So one metaphor for spring is "the flowering of paradox." As spring's wonders arise from winter's hardships, we are invited to reflect on the many "both-ands" we must hold to live life fully and well—and to become more confident that as creatures embedded in nature, we know in our bones how to hold them.

The deeper our faith, the more doubt we must endure; the deeper our hope, the more prone we are to despair; the deeper our love, the more pain its loss will bring: these are a few of the paradoxes we must hold as human beings. If we refuse to hold them in hopes of living without doubt, despair, and pain, we also find ourselves living without faith, hope, and love. But in the spring we are reminded that human nature, like nature herself, can hold opposites together as paradoxes, resulting in a more capacious and generous life.[5]

Summer is the season of abundance and first harvest. Having traced the seed of true self on its arduous journey from birth, through death and dormancy, into flowering, we can look at the abundance that has grown up within us and ask, "Whom is this meant to feed? Where am I called to give my gifts?" In the summer of our lives, we learn more about *whose* we are, rooted in our knowledge of *who* we are.[5]

The idealists among us tend to ask the "whose" question prematurely: we want to serve the world's needs, but we burn out trying to do more than we are able. I cannot give what I do not possess, so I need to know what gifts have grown up within me that are now ready to be harvested and shared. If the gifts I give are mine, grown from the seed of true self, I can give them without burning out. Like the fruit of a tree, they will replenish themselves in due season.

A circle of trust that follows the cycle of the seasons can help us become gardeners of our own souls. It can teach us what every good gardener knows—that life is a constant interplay between the powers within us, for which we are responsible, and the powers outside us, over which we have little control. As we learn the choreography of life that Thomas Merton called "the general dance"— a cocreative process in which we sometimes lead and sometimes follow—we can participate in it with more confidence and grace.[6]

In the midst of our diverse beliefs and disbeliefs, the seasonal metaphors have the power to host an open but focused inquiry into our inner lives. Why? Because beneath our varied convictions, we share something much deeper than belief: creaturely lives embedded in the natural world and cycles of experience that echo the rhythms of nature. The metaphors of the seasons evoke our common condition, allowing us to explore it in ways that both challenge and comfort us.[7]

I have heard people claim that genuine dialogue is becoming impossible in our society, whose common ground seems to shrink as its diversity grows. But in the space created by seasonal metaphors, the impossible can happen.

I have seen a secular Jewish professor, who is alienated from all things religious, sitting across the circle from an African American schoolteacher who belongs to a Holiness Pentecostal church. I have listened to these two explore matters of deep meaning, each speaking in a language of personal integrity. I have watched them receive each other with openness and respect, and I have sensed them becoming even more open in the process.

In our wounded world, a dialogue of this sort is a miracle of communion—a miracle made possible by metaphors that evoke the hidden wholeness of our lives.

✿❧ Graceful Ambiance ❦✿

There is one more condition that helps make a circle of trust attractive to the soul and to people who are snared by catch-22. We must gather in settings and be guided by schedules that possess simple grace.

We often meet in places so ugly that they repel the soul—and anyone who spends much time at hotel conference centers knows what I mean. The rooms have ceilings that are either too high or too low; few, if any, windows; harsh lighting that turns people green; uncomfortable chairs in rows, sometimes bolted to the floor; hard surfaces that echo with sound; heating or cooling systems that make so much "white noise" people can scarcely be heard; and decor that does not merit the name.

We seem to have forgotten that the environment in which we meet has an impact on the quality of what happens within us and between us. Fortunately, there is a simple formula for a setting that welcomes the soul: create an ambiance that is the antithesis of the one I just described!

- Let the room be neither cramped nor cavernous, with enough space to allow for a circle of comfortable chairs that (if the group is large) can easily be moved and gathered into small groups.
- Let there be eye-level windows to provide visual relief and allow the outside world to come in.
- Let the decor be warm and inviting, with simple grace notes such as fresh flowers.
- Let there be carpet on the floor so the sound does not bounce around and acoustics that permit soft voices to be heard by all.
- Let the lighting be incandescent and warm, not fluorescent and cold.

The schedule for a circle of trust has as much to do with welcoming the soul as the beauty of our surroundings. Physical space and the flow of time both have an aesthetic to which the soul responds: grace in scheduling is the counterpart to physical comfort and warmth.

But *graceless* is the word that best describes many schedules. Jam-packed with things that must be done if we are to justify this use of time, our meetings take us on forced marches from one topic to the next, making it impossible to explore anything deeply and well. We go crashing through the forest together, harried and breathless, staying on the surface with our intellects and egos, while all things soulful flee deeper into the woods.

There are three keys to creating a schedule that welcomes the soul: slow down, do more with less, and pay attention to rhythm. Here, for example is the schedule for the first half of a daylong gathering of an ongoing circle of trust—a schedule whose main elements I will examine in the next few chapters.

We gather on a Saturday at 9:00 A.M., starting out with three or four minutes of silence. Then the facilitator invites us to take fifteen minutes in self-selected groups of three to check in with each other around the question "Since our last gathering, what has happened in your life that you would like others to know about?"

When the small groups end, the facilitator hands out a poem to focus the morning's dialogue on the topic of the day. The topic is "the seed of true self," and the poem is "Love After Love" by Derek Wolcott:

> *The time will come*
> *when, with elation,*
> *you will greet yourself arriving*
> *at your own door, in your own mirror,*
> *and each will smile at the other's welcome,*
> *and say, sit here. Eat.*
> *You will love again the stranger who was your self.*
> *Give wine. Give bread. Give back your heart*
> *to itself, to the stranger who has loved you*
> *all your life, whom you ignored*
> *for another, who knows you by heart.*
> *Take down the love letters from the bookshelf,*
> *the photographs, the desperate notes,*
> *peel your own image from the mirror.*
> *Sit. Feast on your life.*[8]

The poem occupies only half a page, but it will occupy us for the next two and a half hours. During the first hour, the facilitator guides a communal inquiry into the poem, and the topic, by asking questions that allow us to explore with each other both the text and our own experience. Then he or she calls for a silent break of thirty minutes, giving us a chance to reflect on what we have heard and said by taking a walk, writing in a journal, or whatever the soul requires.

Next the facilitator invites us to gather for forty-five minutes in self-selected groups of three. There is to be no "ping-pong" conversation in these groups, with people bouncing ideas and experiences back and forth. Instead, each member of the triad is given fifteen minutes of focus from the other two, a chance to deepen and personalize his or her exploration of the topic.

Finally, the facilitator invites us back to the large circle for fifteen minutes of sharing issues and insights that have emerged from both our solo and small-group explorations. Then we have lunch, followed by a two-hour solitary, silent break before the circle regathers in midafternoon to take a next step.

Instead of larding the schedule with multiple topics and lengthy texts, we have spent most of the morning focused on a single topic, framed by a brief poem. We have created a space that honors diverse learning styles, and souls, by moving from large group exploration to solitude and silence to small group dialogue and back to the large group again.

Slow down, do more with less, and pay attention to rhythm. In crafting a schedule for a circle of trust, this is what it means to walk into the woods quietly, sit at the base of a tree, and wait patiently for the shy soul to emerge and make its claim on our lives.

CHAPTER VI

The Truth Told Slant

The Power of Metaphor

Tell all the Truth but tell it slant—
Success in Circuit lies
Too bright for our infirm Delight
The Truth's superb surprise
—EMILY DICKINSON[1]

❧ Now I Become Myself ❧

I do not know who coined the phrase "Every day, in every way, I am getting better and better," but he or she must have had a great fantasy life. In sixty-five years on earth, my pattern has never been onward and upward. It has always been up and down and back around. I follow the thread of true self faithfully for a while. Then I lose it and find myself back in the dark, where fear drives me to search for the thread once again.

That pattern, as far as I can tell, is inherent in the human condition. Yet its grip on my life has weakened as I have explored it in circles of trust. Today, I lose the thread less often than I once did and find it sooner when I do. But to deal with my recidivism, I first had to stop denying it and then stop generalizing about it, the kind of generalizing I am doing here! I had to acknowledge and examine those autobiographical details where the devil—and God—can be found, details that I often find too painful to talk about openly.

In deference to such feelings, and to the shy soul, a circle of trust does not run headlong at topics like losing and finding true self. Here people are not asked, as I was once asked at a retreat, to "get into pairs and tell each other something shameful about yourself that you have never told anyone"! Instead, the facilitator guides an exploration of the topic by means of a poem, a story, a piece of music, or a work of art—any metaphorical embodiment that allows us to approach the topic indirectly.

Here, for example, are the opening lines of May Sarton's "Now I Become Myself":

Now I become myself. It's taken
Time, many years and places;

I have been dissolved and shaken,
Worn other people's faces,
Run madly, as if Time were there,
Terribly old, crying a warning,
"Hurry, you will be dead before—"
(What? Before you reach the morning?
Or the end of the poem is clear?
Or love safe in the walled city?)[2]

As we discuss these lines in a circle of trust, we conduct an indirect exploration of losing and finding true self. For a while, it may sound as if we are talking about the poet's journey toward selfhood. But we soon come to understand that whatever we say about the poem, we are saying about ourselves. We are reflecting on our own histories of disguising ourselves as someone else, on our own moments of being "dissolved and shaken" as a prelude to self-discovery, on our own fear of dying before we know who we are, and on the frenzy that fear creates within us.

None of these topics is easy, and some we would prefer to avoid. But by addressing them via a poem, we can hold them at whatever distance we choose while staying focused on meaningful matters. As our communal dialogue continues—as we learn that this space is focused, meaningful, revealing, and yet profoundly safe—we develop the trust to speak more directly about ourselves. The shy soul emerges more frequently and needs less protective cover to speak.

🙿 Success in Circuit Lies 🙾

Every practice that creates a circle of trust must keep the space between us open and free and yet focused on things of the soul. We must be intentional about exploring the real issues of our lives:

faith and fear, hope and despair, love and hate, among others. But our explorations must be invitational, giving everyone the freedom to engage those issues in his or her own way. When our intentionality becomes heavy-handed or our openness becomes aimless, the soul will not show up.

How do we create a space that is both focused and inviting? Emily Dickinson—she of the notoriously shy soul—offers invaluable guidance:

> *Tell all the Truth but tell it slant—*
> *Success in Circuit lies*
> *Too bright for our infirm Delight*
> *The Truth's superb surprise*
>
> *As Lightning to the Children eased*
> *With explanation kind*
> *The Truth must dazzle gradually*
> *Or every man be blind—*[3]

In Western culture, we often seek truth through confrontation. But our headstrong ways of charging at truth scare the shy soul away. If soul truth is to be spoken and heard, it must be approached "on the slant." I do not mean we should be coy, speaking evasively about subjects that make us uncomfortable, which weakens us and our relationships. But soul truth is so powerful that we must allow ourselves to approach it, and it to approach us, indirectly. We must invite, not command, the soul to speak. We must allow, not force, ourselves to listen.

We achieve *intentionality* in a circle of trust by focusing on an important topic. We achieve *indirection* by exploring that topic metaphorically, via a poem, a story, a piece of music, or a work of art that embodies it. I call these embodiments "third things" because they represent neither the voice of the facilitator nor the voice of a participant. They have voices of their own, voices that tell the truth about a topic but, in the manner of metaphors, tell it on the slant. Mediated by a third thing, truth can emerge from, and return to, our awareness at whatever pace and depth we are able to handle—sometimes inwardly in silence, sometimes aloud in community—giving the shy soul the protective cover it needs.

Rightly used, a third thing functions a bit like the old Rorschach inkblot test, evoking from us whatever the soul wants us to attend to. Mediated by a good metaphor, the soul is more likely than usual to have something to say. But that fact will count for nothing if we fail to recognize that the soul is speaking or fail to pay attention to what it says.

This is why an unconventional kind of note-taking is helpful in a circle of trust. Normally, at workshops and retreats, we take the most notes on what the leader says, the second most on what certain interesting people in the group say, and few, if any, notes on the words we ourselves speak. In a circle of trust, we reverse that order, taking the most notes on the words that arise within us, whether we speak them or not.

At first, it seems odd to take notes on our own thoughts and words. We have a strange conceit that just because we have thought or said something, we understand what it means! But in a circle of trust, the inner teacher may give us insights so new or challenging that they take time to understand—insights we may misinterpret, forget, or even deny if we do not record and continue to reflect on them. The notes we take on our own words in such moments become a text that we can learn from long after the circle has ended.

Conversations in which we speak and hear truth on the slant are always at risk because they defy conventional norms. As we explore a May Sarton poem, for example, we may discover (as I once did) that a member of the group did his doctoral dissertation on Sarton. After listening to people talk about the poem for a while, he proclaimed, "What you have been saying is *not* what Sarton had in mind!" Instantly, the circle became unsafe as this "expert" tried to dominate it with "objective" knowledge, intimidating people who had been speaking from their hearts.

In such a moment, the facilitator must move gently—but quickly and firmly—to make everyone feel safe again, including, if possible, the person who made things unsafe. I recall saying something along these lines: "What Sarton had in mind is certainly an interesting topic, but it is not our topic here. Our focus is on how this poem intersects our own lives and evokes our own experience. I invited all of you to speak about the poem in that spirit, and I invite you to continue to do so."

But keeping the circle open to subjective viewpoints does not mean that "anything goes," another way of saying that we must be intentional as well as invitational. A third thing, in the hands of a good facilitator, provides the boundaries that can help keep our exploration in that creative space between aimless meandering and a forced march toward some predetermined goal.

When people wander from a topic and make comments unrelated to it (often because the topic is touching some nerve), the facilitator can call them back to the boundaries of the text itself, asking them to anchor whatever they say in a word, image, or line from the story or the poem. As we are brought back to the text, we are also brought back to the issue—and to the voice of the inner teacher. Now our exploration is more likely to be driven by the agenda of the soul than by the agendas of ego and intellect lurking in the room.

What T. S. Eliot said about poetry is true of all third things: "[Poetry] may make us . . . a little more aware of the deeper, unnamed feelings which form the substratum of our being, to which we rarely penetrate; for our lives are mostly a constant evasion of ourselves."[4]

❧ A Taoist Tale ❧

Over the past thirty years, I have used hundreds of third things while facilitating circles of trust.[5] One of them—a Taoist tale called "The Woodcarver"—has long meant the most to me.[6] It comes to us from the teachings of Chuang Tzu, a Chinese master who lived twenty-five hundred years ago, but it has timeless relevance for anyone on the journey toward an undivided life.

I have two reasons for exploring this story here in some detail. First, doing so gives me a way to illustrate some important features of working with a third thing. Second, it gives all of us a chance to learn more about life on the Möbius strip from Chuang Tzu, a teacher with extraordinary insight into that life's ins and outs.

The Woodcarver

Khing, the master carver, made a bell stand
Of precious wood. When it was finished,
All who saw it were astounded. They said it must be
The work of spirits.
The Prince of Lu said to the master carver:
"What is your secret?"

Khing replied: "I am only a workman:
I have no secret. There is only this:
When I began to think about the work you commanded
I guarded my spirit, did not expend it
On trifles, that were not to the point.
I fasted in order to set
My heart at rest.

After three days fasting,
I had forgotten gain and success.
After five days
I had forgotten praise or criticism.
After seven days
I had forgotten my body
With all its limbs.

"By this time all thought of your Highness
And of the court had faded away.
All that might distract me from the work
Had vanished.
I was collected in the single thought
Of the bell stand.

"Then I went to the forest
To see the trees in their own natural state.
When the right tree appeared before my eyes,
The bell stand also appeared in it, clearly, beyond doubt.
All I had to do was to put forth my hand
And begin.

"If I had not met this particular tree
There would have been
No bell stand at all.

"What happened?
My own collected thought
Encountered the hidden potential in the wood;
From this live encounter came the work
Which you ascribe to the spirits."

Here, in print, it is impossible to reproduce the communal dialogue this story usually generates, impossible to do more than hint at the power of such a dialogue to illumine, affirm, and question our lives. Here the complex and probing discourse that would go on in a circle of trust gets reduced to a single voice: mine. So your imagination will be required to redeem what follows.

Imagine that you are sitting in a circle with twenty people, each of whom has a copy of "The Woodcarver" in hand. The facilitator asks questions to guide a dialogue; people respond, some inwardly, some aloud, often allowing brief silences to fall between speakers; laughter as well as solemnity is laced through the conversation; and together we weave a fabric of meanings about both the story and our own lives. As I describe this communal process, imagine that you are part of it, and let the woodcarver's story evoke your own.

The facilitator begins by asking if someone, whoever wishes, will read the first stanza aloud, someone else the second, and so on until the whole story has been told. Hearing the story read aloud in several voices, with their varied inflections and emphases, hints at the rich potential of the communal process.

Then the facilitator asks an overview question that allows people to offer first takes on the text as a whole: "What is this story about for you? How does it intersect your life at this moment? Is there a word, a phrase, or an image here that speaks directly to your condition?"

After some silence, someone says, "I am a teacher. I don't work with wood, but I see parallels here to my work with children. I really want to help all of my students find the 'bell stand' within themselves." Another says, "The story makes me think of my work. I am constantly under pressure to produce results, just like the woodcarver. And it is really getting to me." Yet another says, "I need some way of stepping back from everyday demands to reflect more deeply on what I am doing, the way the woodcarver did. But I just can't seem to do it. I envy this guy's chance to be contemplative."

As people speak about ways in which the story intersects their lives, at least two things happen. People who speak may hear themselves naming truths they have not named before—and even if they have, naming them in front of others helps the speaker take them more seriously. People who listen, even if they do not speak, may hear someone give voice to a truth that is *their* truth as well, one that they would never have thought to name for themselves. Whether we speak or listen or do both, exploring inner life issues in community, via a third thing, can yield important insights.

My own speaking and listening in many circles of trust have given me some insights into how the woodcarver's tale illumines my life. As a facilitator-participant, I might say something like this:

> Like me, Khing is under pressure to be concerned only about externals: the prince and his command, the product he is supposed to deliver, the tools and materials available to him, the way others evaluate his work. But he turns away from these externals toward inner truth—not to escape the world but to return to it in a way that will allow him to cocreate something of worth and beauty.
>
> He makes this inward turn in a very stressful situation! The command to make the bell stand came from a prince who rules over a workplace that has no personnel handbook and no grievance procedure. Suppose Khing had messed up: the Prince might have had him killed. Despite the fear he must have felt, Khing takes the Prince's command and transforms it into a choice.
>
> Of course, not all commands can or should be chosen: some should be resisted unto death! But sometimes I receive commands—from another person or from my life situation—that evoke something from me that I did not know I

had. If I can embrace *that* kind of command and transform it into a choice, good things may happen.

When I became a parent, for example, I did not anticipate the extent to which my life would be "under command" for many years to come. What young parent does? But when I can embrace such a command as a choice, my life becomes larger—as it has from helping to raise three children.

At this point, some people in the circle are nodding in agreement, but others see things quite differently: "Well, I wish I had a boss who would give me seven days off to contemplate my assignment!" Or "I wish I had a job like Khing's, with only one task at a time and with no family responsibilities! After all, this guy didn't have to make the meals, wash the dishes, mow the lawn, and get the car repaired." These people are saying that if their lives were as fancy-free as the woodcarver's, they too could live creatively and with integrity—but in the real world, the woodcarver's path is obviously an impossible dream.

When conflicting viewpoints arise in a circle of trust, we arrive at a critical moment. Now we can easily slip back into business as usual, arguing about whether the real world is as confining as some people suggest, trying to talk each other into, or out of, some opinion. Now we may forget why we are here: not to persuade anyone of anything or to reach consensus on how things really are but to help each person listen to his or her inner teacher.

In such a moment, the facilitator can remind people of the Rorschach inkblot analogy: our responses to "The Woodcarver" say more about us than about the text, so we must pay close attention to what we ourselves are saying. We are not here to debate the story's "objective meaning" (as if it had one) or what the story means for someone else's life (as if we knew). We are here to protect and border and salute each other's solitude, as each of us listens for whatever meanings the story and our dialogue about it may evoke from our own inner teacher.

At the same time, the facilitator needs to remind people that a text has a voice of its own—one that we must listen to as attentively as we listen to other people's voices. In this case, the facilitator might point out that nowhere does this story say that the Prince gave Khing seven days off in order to fast and forget: it simply says that Khing went through a process that took seven days. Nor does the story tell us that Khing abandoned hearth and home to go off on retreat by himself: he might well have done his fasting and forgetting in the midst of his ongoing family, workplace, and civic responsibilities.

Gently but firmly, the facilitator's message must be this: "Whether you find yourself drawn to or repelled by the story or someone else's interpretation of it, simply take note of your response and reflect on it. Ask yourself what personal experiences lie behind it; ask yourself what inner issues you may be projecting. Try to understand your own responses, and you may discover that your inner teacher has something important to say."

After a while, the facilitator no longer needs to remind people about all this. As participants begin to understand that whatever they say about a third thing, they are saying about themselves, the reminders come from within.

Naming Our Own Truth

Having begun by inviting people to explore the story openly for ten or fifteen minutes, the facilitator needs to bring the dialogue into sharper focus, balancing openness with intentionality.

As facilitator, I might say something like this: "Stories such as 'The Woodcarver' always reward close reading, so let's start working our way through the tale step by step. First, let's look at the way Chuang Tzu sets the stage for this drama in the first few lines:

> *Khing, the master carver, made a bell stand*
> *Of precious wood. When it was finished,*
> *All who saw it were astounded. They said it must be*
> *The work of spirits.*
> *The Prince of Lu said to the master carver:*
> *"What is your secret?"*
>
> *Khing replied: "I am only a workman:*
> *I have no secret. . . ."*

"Here Khing is, surrounded by spectators who are dazed by the beauty of the bell stand. The people say, 'It must be the work of spirits.' The Prince asks, 'What is your secret?' and Khing replies, 'I am only a workman: I have no secret.' How do you understand what is going on here? What do you think the parties to this exchange are trying to say to each other?"

One person says that the Prince and the people were simply in awe of the woodcarver's capacity to create beauty. Someone else suggests that they lusted after Khing's "secret" so they could mass-produce and market his work as a Wal-Mart special! Another believes that the Prince was threatened by the woodcarver's powers and was trying to regain the upper hand by uncovering his tricks. Yet another claims that both the Prince and the people were trying to evade the challenge of using their own human gifts by treating the woodcarver as if he were superhuman.

As people speak, we learn at least two things. First, people interpret these opening lines differently because they have different inner issues. Second, just as we are projecting our needs onto the story, so the people in the story are projecting their needs onto the woodcarver! Whether the source of the projections within the story is awe, commercial self-interest, lust for power, or self-abnegation, this much seems clear: as the action gets under way, Khing is surrounded by powerful projections that make him into a magician of some sort.

Surely these projections appealed to Khing's ego. At least, that is *my* response to this Rorschach test! Who would not want to be credited with superhuman abilities? We gladly embrace projections of this sort all the time: it is called professional posturing. "Of course I have a secret. But I spent a lot of time and money to get trained as a doctor (or an accountant or a mechanic), and I'm not about to give my secret away! I may tell you a little about the tricks of my trade, but I will use words so obscure that you will not understand what I am saying!"

Yet Khing resists the projections people lay on him. Why? Because he knows that as soon as we succumb to someone else's definition of who we are, we lose our sense of true self and of our right relation to the world. It makes no difference whether those projections make us the hero or the goat: when we allow others to name us, we lose touch with our own truth and undermine our capacity to cocreate in life-giving ways with "the other."

You do not need to be a master of anything to be caught in a web of projections: you need only live and work with other people! Teachers catch projections when students say, in effect, "You're the expert. Just give us the answers so we don't have to think for ourselves," tempting them to dispense information instead of helping students learn. Writers catch projections when readers say, in effect, "You wrote a book on this subject, so you must be an expert on it," tempting them to lose the edge of not-knowing that animates the best thinking and writing. Parents catch projections from children, bosses from employees, politicians from citizens: the list is endless and the projections are endlessly distorting.

So the woodcarver resists people's efforts to name him from the outside in. With simplicity and clarity, he claims the right to name himself from the inside out: "I am only a workman: I have no secret." When we fail to take this first, critical step of fending off projections and reserving the right to name our own truth, we become lost in eternal smoke and mirrors and cannot even find the trail head of the path into our inner lives.

As we explore the opening movement of "The Woodcarver," questions start to grow for everyone in the circle: What projections surround me? Where do they come from? What drives them? How do they distort my sense of self? How am I dealing with them, and how might I deal with them better? How can I name and claim my own truth? Such questions, and our answers to them, are critical steps on the journey toward an undivided life.

The Work Before the Work

The woodcarver knows that to do good work, he must deal with external constraints without compromising his inner freedom, letting these polarities flow into each other like the surfaces of a Möbius strip. So he begins not by focusing on the job the Prince commanded him to do but on a job much nearer at hand: the inner work of reclaiming true self—a work he does without ceasing as his story unfolds.

As we explore the story in a circle of trust, people realize that Khing, who has been asked how he created such a remarkable work of art, says nothing about the kind of chisel he used, the angle at which he held it, or the amount of pressure he applied as he carved the wood!

One reason for this, of course, is that tools and techniques are second nature to someone who has spent years perfecting his craft. But there is a deeper reason for Khing's silence on the technical aspects of his work: as important as they are, they are not the most challenging aspect of bringing truth and beauty into the world. The real challenge is the one Khing talks about: the formation of the human heart behind the skillful hand.

I call this part of the story "the work before the work"—a phrase I try to remember when I receive a new "command." Before I turn to my work in the world, I have inner work to do:

> *"When I began to think about the work you commanded*
> *I guarded my spirit, did not expend it*
> *On trifles, that were not to the point.*
> *I fasted in order to set*
> *My heart at rest.*
> *After three days fasting,*
> *I had forgotten gain and success.*
> *After five days*
> *I had forgotten praise or criticism.*
> *After seven days*
> *I had forgotten my body*
> *With all its limbs."*

There is a lovely irony in the fact that Khing, who had just proclaimed, "I have no secret," proceeds to reveal what seems to be a secret of the first order by describing the inner journey that took him from the Prince's command to the tree with the bell stand in it. As the facilitator of a circle of trust, I invite people to take this description not as a formula to be followed but as a set of images to stimulate imagination. What are your personal parallels to "guarding" or "fasting" or "forgetting"? What do you do, or wish you could do, to arrive at the inner place Khing comes to before he enters the forest? What is your version of the inner journey toward an undivided life?

Here are some of my own responses to this part of the Rorschach test. Khing describes his first inward step by saying, "I guarded my spirit." This may sound like those illusory second and third phases in the relation of our inner and outer lives—an effort to hide out behind a wall and hold the world at bay. But that is not how Khing describes what he means by "guarding."

He says, "I guarded my spirit, did not expend it / On trifles, that were not to the point." Instead of guarding his spirit against the outside world—a world that is always with us, from which there is no escape—Khing guarded his spirit against his own tendency to expend it on trivia, to respond to external forces with knee-jerk reflexes instead of reflective self-determination.

In particular, Khing guarded himself against the reflex called fear. When he says, "I fasted in order to set my heart at rest," he acknowledges that his heart was fearful when he first received the Prince's command.

As a person well acquainted with fear, I take consolation in the fact that Khing—who has done his work so well for so long that he is called a "master carver"—found himself afraid once again when he got his new assignment! As a young man, I yearned for the day when, rooted in the experience that comes only with age, I could do my work fearlessly. But today, in my mid-sixties, I realize that I will feel fear from time to time for the rest of my life.

I may never get rid of my fear. But like Khing, I can learn to walk into it and through it whenever it rises up. So I watch with fascination as Khing takes the next step on his inner journey: he heightens his awareness of life on the Möbius strip by naming the inner forces that trigger his fear—forces against which he must guard his spirit lest they distort his relation to the outer world. In particular, he names his attraction to "gain and success" and his vulnerability to "praise or criticism."

The world uses punishments and rewards to motivate us, to redirect us, or to keep us in line. But those sanctions cannot work until we internalize them. Only when we assent to the world's logic does it have power over us. So Khing withdraws his assent by "fasting" and "forgetting." Of course, forgetting about gain and success, praise and criticism, is easier said than done. But naming our fears aloud—as Khing does and as we can do in a circle of trust—is a first step toward transcending them.

Then Khing says that he forgot his "body / With all its limbs." People sometimes feel that these words devalue the body, but my response to this Rorschach test is the reverse. Anyone who works at a high level of physical skill—as a good woodcarver, athlete, or instrumentalist does—must trust his or her body implicitly, which is tantamount to "forgetting." A shortstop or concert pianist who wonders for even a split second whether his or her hands are correctly positioned will flub that hard-hit ground ball or falter in the middle of that fast-moving Chopin riff.

When we "forget" the body in this way, we learn the true meaning of the old saying that "the body has a mind of its own." Even those of us who play neither baseball nor a Steinway must learn to trust bodily knowledge as part of our inner guidance. As we do so, we, like the woodcarver, become less responsive to external commands and more responsive to the inner teacher. We start to live in closer conformity to our own souls.

As we explore "the work before the work" in a circle of trust, people wrestle, aloud and in silence, with many important questions about the inner journey:

- How do I guard my spirit? Do I even believe in guarding it, or have I been conditioned simply to give my spirit away?

- What fears paralyze me? Can I name them with the same liberating clarity that Khing names gain and success, praise and criticism, and bodily security?

- What practices do I have that parallel Khing's "fasting" and "forgetting" that could help me move into and through my fears for the sake of reclaiming true self?

As the woodcarver deals with such questions, his journey emerges from the "inside" of the Möbius strip and takes him toward engagement with the "outside" world:

"By this time all thought of your Highness
And of the court had faded away.
All that might distract me from the work
Had vanished.
I was collected in the single thought
Of the bell stand.

"Then I went to the forest
To see the trees in their own natural state.
When the right tree appeared before my eyes,
The bell stand also appeared in it, clearly, beyond doubt.
All I had to do was to put forth my hand
And begin."

Long before the bell stand arrives on the scene, there are three critical outcomes of "the work before the work" that we can explore in a circle of trust, each of them leading to reflection on the parallels in our own lives.

Consider, first, the sheer chutzpah of the woodcarver's words to the Prince: "By this time all thought of your Highness / And of the court had faded away. / All that might distract me from the work / Had vanished." It is as if your boss asked how you managed to do so well with the assignment he or she gave you, and you replied, "Well, frankly, I had to forget that you and this organization even exist!"

Which is, of course, true. When we are attuned to the expectations of the boss or the corporate culture rather than to the soul's imperatives, we cannot cocreate anything of truth and beauty. If that man from the Department of Agriculture had not allowed the thought of his boss and the bureaucracy to fade away for a while, he would never have heard his inner teacher say, "You report to the land."

Second, Khing says, "I was collected in the single thought / Of the bell stand." He does not say (as we might), "I collected my thoughts and came up with the perfect plan for a bell stand." Instead, he uses the passive form of the verb, indicating that he let go of his own intentions and died to his own ego, allowing himself to be gathered up into a larger truth that gave shape to his work. Here, I believe, is the heart of our spiritual yearning: to be connected with something larger and truer than our own egos and their designs.

Third, Khing's inner work takes him into the forest, back to the "outer" world: "Then I went to the forest / To see the trees in their own natural state. . . . / All I had to do was to put forth my hand and begin." The inner journey, pursued faithfully and well, always takes us back to the world of action.

But when we return to that world, we find ourselves in a different place than before we took the inner journey. Now Khing has no anxious and ambitious plans to impose on the trees in the forest. He walks into the woods in possession of his own truth and is thus able to see the true nature of each tree. In one tree he saw the bell stand, "clearly, beyond doubt"—not because he had superior knowledge of trees but because he had superior knowledge of himself.

Work of every sort has its equivalent to the woodcarver's tree. For the parent, it is a child; for the teacher, a student; for the manager, an employee; for the writer, words; for the mechanic, a machine.[7] When we do not see ourselves clearly, we can see the other only "through a glass, darkly." But when we are clear about our own identities, as the woodcarver is about his, we can be clearer about the identity of the other as well. And from this truer knowing emerges truer cocreation.

❧ This Live Encounter ☙

Having said, "All I had to do was to put forth my hand / And begin," Khing ends his story this way:

> *"If I had not met this particular tree*
> *There would have been*
> *No bell stand at all.*

> *"What happened?*
> *My own collected thought*
> *Encountered the hidden potential in the wood;*
> *From this live encounter came the work*
> *Which you ascribe to the spirits."*

With the words "If I had not met this particular tree / There would have been / No bell stand at all," Khing challenges the conceit at the heart of our concept of professionalism. I mean the conceit that—given sound knowledge, skillful means, and the power to impose our will—we can always get the desired results from the "raw materials" of the world.

Khing knows differently. Like every good gardener, potter, teacher, and parent, he understands that the "other" with which we work is never mere raw material to be formed into any shape we choose. Every "other" we work with has its own nature, its own limits and potentials, with which we must learn to cocreate if we hope to get real results. Good work is relational, and its outcomes depend on what we are able to evoke from each other.

At the heart of this story is a truth that took me a long time to see, partly because it is unspoken, partly because it makes me nervous: for the bell stand to be created, the tree had to be cut down. The bell stand would not have emerged had Khing been unwilling to take a saw to the tree and leave sawdust on the forest floor.

I find constant parallels to this fact in my own work as a teacher. Now and then I meet a student in whom I think I see a bell stand, some marvelous gift that the student has not yet seen or brought into being. Sometimes my effort to release that bell stand—though difficult for both the student and me—eventually brings both of us joy, because the student is ready and willing to name and claim his or her gift.

But at other times, the "cutting" I do leads only to pain, for one of two reasons. Sometimes the student has a bell stand inside but fights the process of releasing it. This student is not ready to embrace his or her gift—and I am the man in the Kazantzakis story who tries to force life upon the butterfly! And sometimes the student does not have what I thought I saw. I have projected a gift that is not there because my ego wants that student to be someone he or she is not, perhaps to prove what a "good teacher" I am. In this case, if I fail to withdraw my false projection in time, I may do the student real harm.

Good work is risky business. When failure compels me to recognize those risks, I can easily become paralyzed by fear—reverting, for example, to the safety of teaching by rote rather than relationship. At such moments, there is one line in "The Wood-carver" that speaks to me as deeply as any other: "All I had to do was to put forth my hand / And begin." Once one has known failure, the very act of putting forth your hand and beginning again can be an act of real courage!

But Khing's final words invite us beyond fear, back to the hopeful heart of the matter: "From this live encounter came the work / Which you ascribe to the spirits." Live encounters are partnerships in which the full powers of two or more beings are at play: the woodcarver and the tree, the teacher and the student, the leader and the led. Helping more of these partnerships happen in our lives is what this story is about for me.

Live encounters are unpredictable, challenging, and risky. They carry no guarantees, so they are much less popular than those "inert collisions" in which we treat each other as objects. But live encounters offer us something that inert collisions lack: they are full of the vitality that makes life worth living, and they enhance our odds of doing worthy work.

As we end our exploration of "The Woodcarver" in a circle of trust, we emerge with a heightened awareness of life on the Möbius strip. The inner teacher has been stimulated by reflective and respectful dialogue, yielding insights that might not have come to us had we been alone with the tale. But once we have explored the story in a circle of trust, the woodcarver himself can become a companion on our continuing journey. When a third thing comes alive for us in community, we can carry on a dialogue with it long after the circle has disbanded.

Or so it has been for me with Khing, the woodcarver, a character from whom I have received much guidance since I first met him in community some thirty years ago. He is available to me in every moment of daily life, having been rendered so vivid in my imagination by so many circles of trust.

CHAPTER VII

Deep Speaks to Deep

Learning to Speak and Listen

And so I appeal to a voice, to something shadowy,
a remote important region in all who talk:
though we could fool each other, we should consider—
lest the parade of our mutual life get lost in the dark.
—WILLIAM STAFFORD[1]

❧ A Tale of the Inner Teacher ❧

Approaching soul truth "on the slant" through the use of third things helps create a circle of trust. But we make or break that circle by the way we speak, listen, and respond to each other about a poem, a topic, a feeling, or a problem. Here we are governed by that simple but countercultural rule, "No fixing, no saving, no advising, no setting each other straight." I want to tell a story about how difficult—and revelatory—abiding by that rule can be.

In a racially diverse circle of trust, there was a white middle school teacher, Janet, who sat through the first retreat in silence, looking angry and distracted. No one invaded Janet by asking her what was wrong or evaded her by pretending she was not there. Instead, people went on with their dialogue while remaining present and open to her, waiting for her soul to appear.

At the start of the second retreat, as the group explored a poem that touched on racial issues, Janet's grievances began to spill out. She was having a terrible time in her classroom, and it was all the fault of "those students," and all of "those students" were black. But no one invaded Janet by challenging her about racism or evaded her by pretending she was not there—this despite the fact that there were a number of teachers in the circle, black and white, who must have been deeply upset about what their colleague was saying. Instead, everyone continued to wait for Janet's soul.

Sometimes Janet's grievances were received in respectful silence before someone said something else about the poem. Occasionally, someone responded to her with an honest, open question, giving her an opportunity to explore the situation—"What first happened that made you feel this way?" or "What do you find most difficult about so-and-so?"—though Janet almost always used such questions, not to explore, but to expand on her complaints.

From time to time, other teachers spoke of binds they had gotten into with their students, and a couple of black teachers told stories of their own struggles with students who happened to be white. These stories were told, not in judgment of Janet, but as honest testimony to the fact that we are all in this together. And one story involved such a hilarious moment of cultural "crossed wires" that this heavy topic became a little lighter for a while.

Janet struggled with her demons during the second and third retreats. Then, at the fourth retreat, something remarkable happened. Speaking through tears, Janet told the group that after the last retreat, she had become appalled at what she had heard herself saying. She had resolved to build a better relationship with her most difficult student and had learned things about his life that turned some of her anger to compassion. Her classroom troubles had diminished as she acted on the insight that a big part of the problem came from inside of her.

There are times, of course, when we need to confront scourges such as racism head-on. But confrontation often falls short of transformation: some people are coerced into short-lived "changes of heart," while others cling more tightly to the errors of their ways. Janet's transformation was deep and abiding because it came from within, made possible by a community that trusted her inner teacher and allowed her to hear its voice.

🌿 Why Do We Want to Help? 🌿

"No fixing, no saving, no advising, no setting each other straight." The rule is simple, but abiding by it is hard work for people accustomed to straightening each other out as a way of life. Once when I introduced the rule at the start of a long-term circle, someone blurted out, "Then what in heaven's name *are* we going to do with each other for the next two years? You've just excluded the only things we know how to do!"

And that, as they say, is no joke, especially for those of us in the so-called helping professions, who sometimes act as if our entire reason for being is to set other people straight. I recently facilitated a session where one participant was so certain that another's mortal soul depended on her advice—rules be damned!—that I had to ask her three times to cease and desist.

So what *do* we do in a circle of trust? We do what the people in Janet's circle did: we speak our own truth; we listen receptively to the truth of others; we ask each other honest, open questions instead of giving counsel; and we offer each other the healing and empowering gifts of silence and laughter.

This way of being together is so countercultural that it requires clear explanation, steady practice, and gentle but firm enforcement by a facilitator who can keep us from reverting to business as usual. But once we have experienced it, we want to take this way of being into other relationships, from friendship and the family to the workplace and civic life.

If we are to embrace the spirit as well as the letter of the law that governs a circle of trust, we need to understand why the habit of fixing, saving, advising, and setting each other straight has such a powerful grip on our lives. There are times, of course, when that habit is benign, when what grips us is simple compassion. You have a problem, you share it with me, and wanting to help, I offer you counsel in the hope that it will be useful. So far, so good.

But the deeper your issue goes, the less likely it is that my advice will be of any real value. I may know how to fix your car or help you write a paper, but I do not know how to salvage your failing career, repair your broken marriage, or save you from despair. My answer to your deepest difficulties merely reflects what I would do if I were you, which I am not. And even if I were your psychospiritual clone, my solution would be of little use to you unless it arose from within your soul and you claimed it as your own.

In the face of our deepest questions—the kind we are invited to explore in circles of trust—our habit of advising each other reveals its shadow side. If the shadow could speak its logic, I think it would say something like this: "If you take my advice, you will surely solve your problem. If you take my advice but fail to solve your problem, you did not try hard enough. If you fail to take my advice, I did the best I could. So I am covered. No matter how things come out, I no longer need to worry about you or your vexing problem."

The shadow behind the "fixes" we offer for issues that we cannot fix is, ironically, the desire to hold each other at bay. It is a strategy for abandoning each other while appearing to be concerned. Perhaps this explains why one of the most common laments of our time is that "no one really sees me, hears me, or understands me." How can we understand another when instead of listening deeply, we rush to repair that person in order to escape further involvement? The sense of isolation and invisibility that marks so many lives—not least the lives of young people, whom we constantly try to fix—is due in part to a mode of "helping" that allows us to dismiss each other.

When you speak to me about your deepest questions, you do not want to be fixed or saved: you want to be seen and heard, to have your truth acknowledged and honored. If your problem is soul-deep, your soul alone knows what you need to do about it, and my presumptuous advice will only drive your soul back into the woods. So the best service I can render when you speak to me about such a struggle is to hold you faithfully in a space where you can listen to your inner teacher.

But holding you that way takes time, energy, and patience. As the minutes tick by, with no outward sign that anything is happening for you, I start feeling anxious, useless, and foolish, and I start thinking about all the other things I have to do. Instead of keeping the space between us open for you to hear your soul, I fill it up with advice, not so much to meet your needs as to assuage my anxiety and get on with my life. Then I can disengage from you, a person with a troublesome problem, while saying to myself, "I tried to help." I walk away feeling virtuous. You are left feeling unseen and unheard.

How do we change these deeply embedded habits of fixing, saving, advising, and setting each other straight? How do we learn to be present to each other by speaking our own truth; listening to the truth of others; asking each other honest, open questions; and offering the gifts of laughter and silence? These ways of being together are so important in a circle of trust that each of them has its own chapter in this book. This chapter is devoted to learning to speak and listen; Chapter VIII, to the art of asking honest, open questions; and Chapter IX, to the clarifying and healing power of silence and laughter.

Talking to Ourselves

What does it mean to "speak our own truth" in a circle of trust? Of course, the question cannot be answered in terms of the content, which will vary vastly depending on who is speaking and when.

But no matter what the content may be, speaking our truth in a circle of trust always takes the same form: we speak *from* our own center *to* the center of the circle—to the receptive heart of the communal space—where what we say will be held attentively and respectfully. This way of speaking differs markedly from everyday conversations in which we speak *from* our own intellect or ego directly *to* the intellect or ego of someone on whom we hope to have an impact.

Everyday speech is "instrumental" rather than "expressive," intended to achieve a goal rather than simply to tell one's own truth. When we speak instrumentally, we try to influence the listener by informing or affirming or rebuking or making common cause. But when we speak expressively, we speak to express the truth within us, honoring the inner teacher by letting it know that we are attending to its voice. Our purpose is not to teach anyone anything but to give the inner teacher a chance to teach us.

Of course, knowing when we are speaking from the soul rather than the intellect or ego is difficult, since the intellect and ego insist that *they* are the center of our lives and *they* speak the voice of truth! It takes time to learn to distinguish between the various voices within us and even more time to get regular access to the voice of soul. The signs that we are speaking *from* that inward center are subtle, as subtle as the stillness of a pond; the capacity to recognize them grows slowly as we speak in a space where no one is making ripples.

Though it is hard to know when we are speaking *from* our own center, it is not so hard to know when we are speaking *to* the center of the circle: expressive speaking is less stressful than its instrumental counterpart. When we speak directly to others in order to achieve a goal, we feel the anxiety that comes from trying to exercise influence. But when we speak to the center of the circle—free of the need to achieve a result—we feel energized and at peace. Now we speak with no other motive than to tell the truth, and the self-affirming feelings that accompany such speech reinforce the practice.

How we *listen* in a circle of trust is as important as how we speak. When someone speaks from his or her center to the center of the circle, the rest of us may not respond the way we normally do—with affirmations or rebuttals or some other way of trying to influence the speaker. So we learn to take in whatever is said with as much simple receptivity as we can muster.

Receptive listening is an inward and invisible act. But in a circle of trust, it has at least three outward and visible signs:

- Allowing brief, reflective silences to fall between speakers, rather than rushing to respond—silences that honor those who speak, give everyone time to absorb what has been said, and slow things down enough so that anyone who wishes to speak can do so

- Responding to the speaker not with commentary but with honest, open questions that have no other intent than to help the speaker hear more deeply whatever he or she is saying—a demanding art that is the subject of the next chapter

- Honoring whatever truth-telling has been done by speaking one's own truth openly into the center of the circle—placing it alongside prior expressions as simple personal testimony, with no intent of affirming or negating other speakers

When people speak instrumentally, trying to get leverage on each other, it is nearly impossible to listen receptively to what another says. We listen with half a mind, at best, busily filtering what we hear so that we can embrace what we agree with and reject the rest. We listen, that is, with our egos. But when people speak expressively, we listen openly, with our souls. Now we can attend fully to whatever is being said, knowing that people are not trying to comment on us and our truth but are making an honest effort to express truths of their own.

As we grow in our ability to listen this way, we give the gift of "hearing each other into speech."[2] As *our listening* becomes more open—and speakers start to trust that they are being heard by people whose only desire is to make it safe for everyone to tell the truth—*their speaking* becomes more open as well.

Like every gift given, this one returns as a gift to the giver: when we learn how to listen more deeply to others, we can listen more deeply to ourselves. This may be the most important result of the unconventional speaking and listening that go on in a circle of trust.

When our discourse is aimed at influencing other people, we dare not listen too carefully to our own words—let alone be self-critical about them—lest we start to doubt their validity, become embarrassed by their implications, or otherwise lose the leverage we seek. But as we are liberated from adversarial speaking and listening, we are much more likely to hear and reflect on things we ourselves have said. Now we have the disarming experience of being taught by our own inner teacher!

When I speak from my own center to the center of the circle—in the presence of listeners who neither affirm nor negate what I say—my words simply sit there in the space between us, in full view of everyone, including me. Now I am much more likely to have inner colloquies in which I am questioned or challenged or affirmed. They may come in the middle of a meeting, during a meal, or when I awaken at night:

- "Why did I say *that* when I don't really believe it?"

- "I believe what I said, but I am really not sure what it means."

- "I've known for a long time that what I said is true for me, but I had not understood *how* true it is until just now."

- "As I look at the truth I spoke, I suddenly see implications for my life that I had never seen before."

Many of us have been in settings where there are ground rules to govern speaking and listening. In therapy groups, for example, we are asked to give speakers feedback so that they can understand the emotional impact their words have on others. In "appreciative inquiry" groups, we are asked to paraphrase what we hear speakers say to find out whether we understand what they really mean. These rules can serve good ends in their native settings, but they will undermine the integrity of a circle of trust.

Here it does not matter how listeners are affected by what the speaker says (except when someone violates the circle's rules). Nor does it matter whether listeners understand what the speaker intended to say. In a circle of trust, the only "feedback" that counts is that which comes from within the speaker, and the only understanding that counts is the speaker's own. All that matters here is that we hold each other in a space where the soul feels safe enough to speak its truth—and we feel safe enough to become more receptive to the implications of that truth for our lives.

What happens within us in a circle of trust takes us well beyond narcissistic self-absorption or the fruitless recycling of self-referencing thought. We have a conversation with our own souls—one that just might change our lives.

Telling Our Stories

When the space between us is made safe for the soul by truthful speaking and receptive listening, we are able to speak truth in a particularly powerful form—a form that goes deeper than our opinions, ideas, and beliefs. I mean the truth that emerges as we tell the stories of our lives. As the writer Barry Lopez has noted, truth cannot "be reduced to aphorism or formulas. It is something alive and unpronounceable. Story creates an atmosphere in which [truth] becomes discernible as a pattern."[3]

Storytelling has always been at the heart of being human because it serves some of our most basic needs: passing along our traditions, confessing failings, healing wounds, engendering hope, strengthening our sense of community. But in our culture of invasion and evasion, this time-honored practice cannot be taken for granted. It must be supported in special settings and protected with strong ground rules.

Because our stories make us vulnerable to being fixed, exploited, dismissed, or ignored, we have learned to tell them guardedly or not at all. Neighbors, coworkers, and even family members can live side by side for years without learning much about each other's lives. As a result, we lose something of great value, for the more we know about another's story, the harder it is to hate or harm that person.

Instead of telling our vulnerable stories, we seek safety in abstractions, speaking to each other about our opinions, ideas, and beliefs rather than about our lives. Academic culture blesses this practice by insisting that the more abstract our speech, the more likely we are to touch the universal truths that unite us. But what happens is exactly the reverse: as our discourse becomes more abstract, the less connected we feel. There is less sense of community among intellectuals than in the most "primitive" society of storytellers.

I learned something about the connection between storytelling and community while sitting in a Quaker meeting for worship, a communal silence out of which people occasionally speak. I listened as one man grieved the recent death of his best friend, telling a moving story about an experience the two of them had shared. I did not know this man or his friend, but the story he told took me deep into my own life: it brought my own friends to mind and reminded me of how precious they are and of how important it is that I let them know of that fact.

After ten or fifteen minutes of silence, another person spoke, describing with uncanny accuracy what had happened within me as I listened to the first person speak: "We believe that we will find shared truth by going up into big ideas," she said. "But it is only when we go down, drawing deep from the well of personal experience, that we tap into the living water that supplies all of our lives."

I know of dialogue groups where this principle is given an acid test. People who are at each other's throats over thorny issues like abortion or the death penalty are brought together for a facilitated weekend retreat. During their time together, they are forbidden from announcing, explaining, or defending their position on the issue at hand. Instead, they are invited to tell personal stories about the experiences that brought them to whatever position they hold, while others listen openly.

This process often creates more mutual understanding than other modes of conflict resolution—especially as people are reminded that similar experiences can lead different individuals to very different conclusions. We find common bonds in the shared details of the human journey, not in the divergent conclusions we draw from those details.

Stories are evoked in many ways in a circle of trust. Sometimes they emerge as people make spontaneous connections between the topic being discussed and events in their own lives. Sometimes the facilitator solicits stories of a particular sort: "Tell us about an experience in which you felt a deep sense of community." And sometimes the facilitator invites people to bring stories in the form of "case studies," structured tales of particular life moments that allow us to take a close look at our travels on the Möbius strip.

Teachers, for example, are invited to bring case studies of a good moment and a bad moment in the classroom—a moment when they knew they were "born to teach" and a moment when they "wished they had never been born"—to help them see more clearly how soul and role both come together and fall apart in the course of daily life.[4]

Our personal stories are also evoked by the third things we use to help focus a circle of trust. As we saw in Chapter VI, a story such as "The Woodcarver" or a poem such as "Now I Become Myself" can help us learn from our experience in ways that go much deeper than simply talking about what happened. Archetypal "big stories" such as these shed light on the "little stories" of our lives, revealing meanings that we might otherwise miss.

When we tell our personal stories in a circle of trust, the ground rules prohibit people from helping us "solve" whatever problem may be embedded in those stories. But storytelling in such a circle often yields powerful "solutions" nonetheless—in the lives of those who speak *and* of those who listen.

As a speaker, especially if I talk about things I find shameful or painful, the solution may come from discovering that I can tell my story without being cast into the outer darkness. As I realize that people are receiving my self-revelation without judgment, I find myself freed to dig deeper into the root system of my issue, and the resulting self-knowledge may contain something of the solution I need.

As a listener, I may discover that someone in the circle has a problem similar to mine, and as I hear it voiced in another person's words, I gain new insight into my own dilemma. Sometimes as I hear the person explore a possible resolution to his or her problem, my own inner teacher is evoked. At the very least, knowing that someone else has a problem like mine gives me a sense of not being crazy and alone that in itself can open a path to deeper self-understanding.

A story does not need to become a puzzle with a solution or a fable with a moral in order to do its problem-solving work in our lives. Telling a story expressively, as an end in itself, can contribute powerfully to our insight, healing, and enlivenment. The philosopher Martin Buber pointed to this power in a story about a story:

A story must be told in such a way that it constitutes help in itself. . . . My grandfather was lame. Once they asked him to tell a story about his teacher. And he related how [his teacher] used to hop and dance while he prayed. My grandfather rose as he spoke, and he was so swept away by his story that he began to hop and dance to show how the master had done. From that hour on he was cured of his lameness. That's how to tell a story![5]

What Is Truth?

The soul wants truth, not trivia. So if the space between us is to welcome the soul, it must be a space in which truth can be told. Our ability to create and protect such a space depends on how well we understand the assumptions about truth—and the way truth emerges among us—that form the foundations of a circle of trust.

These assumptions will not find favor with people who believe that there are absolute answers to the deepest questions of our lives and that those who know the answers are obliged to convert everyone else! As the ground rules of a circle of trust make clear—especially the rule that forbids fixing, saving, advising, and setting straight—the arrogance of absolutism is not welcome here.

But neither is the mindlessness of relativism. In fact, the very act of participating in a circle of trust and abiding by its disciplines takes us well beyond the silly and dangerous notion that there is "one truth for you, another truth for me, and never mind the difference." If I believed that, I simply would not bother with this vexatious thing called "community," where I must speak and listen in ways that might alter my understanding of what is true.

You and I may hold different conceptions of truth, but we *must* mind the difference. Whether we know it or not, like it or not, acknowledge it or not, our lives are interconnected in a complex web of causation. My understanding of truth impinges on your life, and yours impinges on mine, so the differences between us matter to both of us. A circle of trust honors both our differences and our connections.

My working definition of truth is simple, though practicing it is anything but: "Truth is an eternal conversation about things that matter, conducted with passion and discipline."[6] Truth cannot possibly be found in the conclusions of the conversation, because the conclusions keep changing. So if we want to live "in the truth," it is not enough to live in the conclusions of the moment. We must find a way to live in the continuing conversation, with all its conflicts and complexities, while staying in close touch with our own inner teacher.

In a circle of trust, we can dwell in the truth by dwelling in the conversation. In such a circle, our differences are not ignored, but neither are they confronted in combat. Instead, they are laid out clearly and respectfully alongside each other. In such a circle, we speak and hear diverse truths in ways that keep us from ignoring each other *and* from getting into verbal shootouts—ways that allow us to grow together toward a larger, emergent truth that reveals how much we hold in common.

How does that larger truth emerge in a circle of trust, and how do we grow toward it? It happens as together we create a "tapestry of truth," a complex fabric of experience and interpretation woven from the diverse threads of insight that each of us brings to the circle. Doing so requires a loom of corporate discipline strong enough to hold those threads in creative tension with one another—a loom provided by the principles and practices of a circle of trust.

According to conventional wisdom, we arrive at shared truth only by confronting and correcting each other in debate. But my experience suggests that we rarely change our minds and move toward mutual understanding in the heat of argument. Instead, we become separated from each other, and from the inner teacher, by our fear of losing the battle—and the energy we expend trying to make sure that we win leaves us with no resources for reflection and transformation.

In combative situations, some people withdraw from the fray, disappearing into foxholes of private belief where the conflict cannot touch them. Others stay on the field and fight by clinging more tightly to some preexisting conviction, wielding it to fend off their foes like the familiar weapon it is. In the midst of intellectual or spiritual warfare, we rarely risk expressing those tentative probes and vulnerable ideas that might lead us to new insights but would also leave us open to attack. Confronted by "the enemy," we become even more committed to whatever we have always believed and are less likely to embrace the challenges that might lead to new understanding.

But in a circle of trust—whose ground rules forbid us from confronting and correcting each other—a remarkable thing happens: we confront and correct ourselves! To put it more precisely, the inner teacher confronts and corrects us. In such a circle, we feel safe enough to put forth tentative and fragile insights. Here we have a chance, over time, to sit quietly with our own and other people's thoughts—a chance to see how our insights relate to the larger pattern of the group and to determine how much of that pattern we wish to embrace as our own.

In a circle of trust, this tapestry of truth is woven continually, right before our eyes. As I watch it emerge, I see places where someone, perhaps me, contributed a thread that seems to enhance the pattern—and places where someone, perhaps me, contributed a thread that now seems discordant. Slowly, organically, my sense of true and false, right and wrong, has a chance to evolve, a fabric of life woven on the loom called a circle of trust. Truth evolves within us, between us, and around us as we participate in "the eternal conversation."

CHAPTER VIII

Living the Questions

Experiments with Truth

*Be patient toward all that is unsolved in your heart
and try to love the questions themselves. . . . Live the
questions now. Perhaps you will then gradually,
without noticing it, live along some distant day into
the answer.*

—RAINER MARIA RILKE[1]

✺ The Truth Beneath My Fear ✺

If we want to create a space that welcomes the soul, we must speak our own truth to the center of the circle and listen receptively as others speak theirs. We must also respond to what others say in ways that extend the welcome, something that rarely happens in daily life.

Listen in on conventional conversations and see how often we respond to each other by agreeing, disagreeing, or simply changing the subject! We do not mean to be inhospitable to the soul, and yet we often are. By inserting our opinions and asserting our agendas, we advance our egos while the speaker's inner teacher retreats.

In a circle of trust, we learn an alternative way to respond, centered on the rare art of asking honest, open questions—questions that invite a speaker to reach for deeper and truer speech. If you do not believe that such questions are rare, just count how many you are asked over the next few days. Honest, open questions are countercultural, but they are vital to a circle of trust. Such questions, asked in a safe space, invite the inner teacher to say more about the matter at hand. And they give the speaker a chance to hear that voice free of the static we create by imposing our predilections on each other.

A few years ago, I became aware of my own need for another talk with the inner teacher. I had entered my early sixties and was feeling anxious about the future, for reasons I did not understand. So I invited a few friends to help me discern what my feelings meant.

The people I called on were experienced and wise, but I did not need their opinions or advice. I needed them to ask me honest, open questions in the hope that I could touch the truth beneath my fear. Guided by the ground rules described in this chapter, they did just that for me. In three two-hour gatherings over a period of eighteen months, they created a space where I was able to discover the source of my anxiety.

Slowly, and with some reluctance, I began to see that what I feared was the impending collision of my age, vocation, and survival. I have worked independently since my late forties, earning my living partly by writing but largely by lecturing and leading workshops around the country. Now, in my early sixties—as I looked down the road at an endless procession of airports, hotel rooms, restaurant food, and auditoriums full of strangers—I worried about my diminishing stamina for this kind of work and about my diminishing income if I were to lay it down.

I was stuck on the horns of that dilemma until the third gathering of my group. I made some comment about aging and fear, and someone responded, "What do you fear most about growing old?" This was not the first time I had been asked that question; in fact, the question was one that I had often asked myself. But this time, my answer came from a place deeper than ego or intellect, in words I had never spoken or even thought: "I fear becoming a seventy-year-old man who does not know who he is when the books are out of print and the audiences are no longer applauding."

The moment I heard those words, I knew I had heard my soul speak—and I knew that I had to act on what I had heard. At stake was not merely my physical and financial comfort but my sense of identity and my spiritual well-being. So I began creating a retirement plan that I am now living into. It is a plan that gives me an opportunity to find out who else might be "in here" besides a writer and a speaker and to act on whatever I may learn while I still have energy and time.

❧ Learning to Ask ❧

I could not have made this decision, with all its attendant risks, without a small group of people whose honest, open questions created a space that invited my soul to speak and allowed me to hear it.

Such questioning may sound easy. But many people, including me, have trouble framing questions that are not advice in disguise. "Have you thought about seeing a therapist?" is *not* an honest, open question! A question like that serves my needs, not yours, pressing you toward my version of your problem and its solution instead of evoking your truth. Many of us need help learning how to ask questions that make the shy soul want to speak up, not shut up.

What are the marks of an honest, open question? An *honest* question is one I can ask without possibly being able to say to myself, "I know the right answer to this question, and I sure hope you give it to me"—which is, of course, what I am doing when I ask you about seeing a therapist. A dishonest question insults your soul, partly because of my arrogance in assuming that I know what you need and partly because of my fraudulence in trying to disguise my counsel as a query.

When I ask you an honest question—for example, "Have you ever had an experience that felt like your current dilemma?" or "Did you learn anything from that prior experience that feels useful to you now?"—there is no way for me to imagine what the "right answer" might be. Your soul feels welcome to speak its truth in response to questions like these because they harbor no hidden agendas.

An *open* question is one that expands rather than restricts your arena of exploration, one that does not push or even nudge you toward a particular way of framing a situation. "How do you feel about the experience you just described?" is an open question. "Why do you seem so sad?" is not.

We all know the difference between open and closed questions, and yet we often slip-slide toward the latter. For example, as I listen to you answer an open question about how you feel, I realize that you have not mentioned anger. Barely aware of what I am doing, I start thinking to myself, "If I were in your situation, I would certainly feel angry . . ."; then I think, "You must be bottling your anger up, and that's not good . . ."; and so I ask you, "Do you feel any anger?"

That question may seem open, since it allows you to answer any way you wish. But because it is driven by my desire to suggest how you *ought* to feel, it is likely to scare your soul away. The fact that I would be angry if I were in your shoes does not mean you have hidden anger; as hard as I may find it to believe, not everyone's inner life is the same as mine! And if you do have hidden anger, my effort to draw it out is likely to make you bury it deeper, as a protection against my presumptuousness. If you are angry, you will deal with it on your timetable, not mine—and step one will be to name your anger for yourself rather than accept my naming of it.

"Try not to get ahead of the language a speaker uses" is a good guideline for asking honest, open questions. By paying close attention to the words people speak, we can ask questions that invite them to probe what they may already know but have not yet fully named. If I ask you, "What did you mean when you said you felt 'frustrated'?" it might help you discover other feelings—if they are there and if you are ready to name them.

But even a question like that will shut you down if I ask it in the hope of getting you to "say the magic word," such as *anger,* that I am expecting to hear! The soul is a highly tuned bunk detector. It is quick to register, and flee from, all attempts at manipulation.

In my own struggle to learn to ask honest, open questions, I find it helpful to have a few guidelines. But the best way to make sure that my questions will welcome the soul is to ask them with an honest, open spirit. And the best way to cultivate that spirit is to remind myself regularly that everyone has an inner teacher whose authority in his or her life far exceeds my own.

The finest school I know for watching the inner teacher at work and learning to ask honest, open questions is a discernment process called the "clearness committee" that has become standard practice in many circles of trust. That name makes it sound like something that came from the sixties, and so it did—the 1660s!

The clearness committee (so named because it helps us achieve clarity) was invented by the early Quakers. As a church that chose to do without benefit of ordained clergy, Quakers needed a structure to help members deal with problems that people in other denominations would simply take to their pastors or priests. That structure had to embody two key Quaker convictions: our guidance comes not from external authority but from the inner teacher, and we need community to help us clarify and amplify the inner teacher's voice.

The clearness committee that resulted is not just a place where we learn to ask honest, open questions. It is a focused microcosm of a larger circle of trust, a setting in which we have an intense experience of what it means to gather in support of someone's inner journey. When clearness committees become a regular part of an ongoing circle of trust, everything else that happens in the circle gains depth—which is why the rest of this chapter is devoted to explaining the clearness process.

❧ Gaining Clarity ❧

The process begins with a "focus person"—someone who is wrestling with an issue related to his or her personal life or work (or both)—inviting four to six people to serve on his or her committee.

"Four to six" is not a casual suggestion: a clearness committee works best with no fewer than four people and no more than six, in addition to the focus person. They should, of course, be people whom the focus person trusts, and when possible, they should represent a variety of backgrounds, experiences, and viewpoints.[2]

Normally, the focus person writes a two- or three-page statement of the problem and gives it to committee members before they meet. If writing does not come easily to the focus person, he or she can tape-record some reflections to share with the committee in advance or make some notes to guide an oral presentation of the problem when the committee gathers.

As a first step toward "clearness," people usually find it helpful to frame the presentation of their problem in three parts:

- *Identifying the problem, as best one is able.* Sometimes the problem is clear ("I have a choice between two job offers"), and sometimes it is vague ("Something is off-center in my life, but I am not really sure what it is"). Since clarity is the aim of the process, the problem itself can be, and often is, murky. And even when the problem seems clear to the focus person, the process may reveal that the real problem is something else!

- *Offering background information that bears directly on the problem.* A modest amount of autobiographical information can help move a clearness committee along. If, for example, you are thinking about leaving your job and you have changed jobs five times in the past decade, you would do well to offer this fact up front.

- *Naming whatever clues there may be on the horizon about where you are headed with the problem.* Here the focus person shares any hunches he or she may have about the issue at hand—whether it is an inclination toward one of those two job offers or simply an anxious feeling about the foggy vista up ahead.

Before the clearness committee begins, members spend some time with the focus person reviewing the rules that govern the process, which will be explained as this chapter proceeds. It is important that everyone understand the rules—as well as the principles behind them—and take seriously the obligation that comes with promising to hold safe space for someone's soul.

Members of the committee should have a printed schedule, modeled on the one presented here, to help them keep the time as well as the rules. Even when the process feels sluggish or the focus person's problem seems to have been resolved, staying with the schedule often yields unexpected insights. So the total time of two hours is nonnegotiable, as is the amount of time allotted for each portion of the process:

7:00 P.M. Sit down in silence in a circle of chairs. The silence will be broken by the focus person when he or she is ready to begin.

7:00–7:15 The focus person describes his or her issue while committee members listen, without interruption.

7:15–8:45 Questions only! For an hour and a half, members of the committee may not speak to the focus person in any way except to ask brief, honest, open questions.

8:45–8:55 Does the focus person want members to "mirror back" what they have heard—in addition to asking more questions—or to continue with questions only? If mirroring is invited, members are to reflect the focus person's words or body language, without interpretation.

8:55–9:00 Affirmations and celebrations of the focus person, each other, and the shared experience.

9:00 P.M. End—remembering to honor the rule of "double confidentiality."

The clearness committee begins with several minutes of silence, which is broken by the focus person when he or she is ready to present the problem. Even when the problem has been shared with committee members in advance, this oral review often reveals nuances that can be conveyed only face to face. The presentation should take no more than fifteen minutes, and during that time, members may not speak, even to ask for clarification.

When the focus person is finished presenting the problem, he or she lets the group members know that their work can begin. For the next ninety minutes, committee members are guided by a simple but demanding rule: *the only way they may speak to the focus person is to ask brief, honest, open questions.*

The questions should be short and to the point, confined to a single sentence, if possible. When I ask a question by saying, "You mentioned such-and-such, which made me think of such-and-such, and so I'd like to ask you such-and-such . . . ," I am often trying to nudge the focus person toward my way of looking at things. A brief question, with no preamble or explanation, reduces the risk that I will start to offer covert advice.

The questions should be gently paced, with periods of silence between a question, a response, and the next question. The clearness committee is not a grilling or a cross-examination; a relaxed and graceful pace helps the shy soul feel safe. If I ask the focus person one question and, after he or she has answered, follow up with another, it is probably all right. But if I am tempted to ask a third question before anyone else has had a chance, I need to take a deep breath and remember that there are other people in the room.

I should not ask questions simply to satisfy my curiosity. Instead, my questions should come from a desire to support the focus person's inner journey with as much purity as I can muster. As a member of the committee, I am not here to get my own needs met. I am here to be fully present to the focus person, hoping to help that person be fully present to his or her soul.

It is usually most helpful to ask questions that are more about the person than about the problem, since a clearness committee is less about problem solving than about drawing close to true self. I remember a committee called by a CEO who was dealing with a complex and painful racial issue in her corporation. She found it helpful when one member asked, "What have you learned about yourself in previous conflicts that might be useful to you now?" But she found it unhelpful when another asked, "Do you have a good corporate lawyer?"

If the focus person feels that a question is not honest and open, he or she has the right to say so, to call a questioner back to the rules and the spirit behind them. But if my question is found wanting, I do *not* have the right to explain or defend myself: "You see, that question came to me when you said such-and-such, then I thought such-and-such, and what I really meant was such-and-such."

Such an "explanation" is just one more way of trying to nudge the focus person toward my way of thinking. If I am challenged by the focus person, I have only one option: to sit back, absorb the critique, and eventually return to the process in a more helpful way. Offering any sort of explanation or defense puts my needs and interests ahead of the focus person's and will scare off his or her soul.

Normally, as questions are asked, the focus person answers them aloud, which helps the person hear whatever the inner teacher is saying. But the focus person has the right to pass on any question, without explanation, and committee members should avoid asking questions of a similar sort. Taking a pass does not mean that the focus person is stifling the inner teacher: he or she may learn something important from the fact that a certain question cannot be answered in front of other people.

❧ No One to Fool but Myself ❧

The discipline of asking honest, open questions is the heart of the clearness committee. But there are other disciplines that guide the committee's work, all of them aimed at supporting the focus person on his or her inner journey.

If the focus person cries, committee members are not free to offer "comfort" by giving the person a tissue, laying a hand on his or her shoulder, or speaking words of consolation. Acts such as these may be compassionate under normal circumstances, but they are disruptive in a clearness committee.

If I try to comfort the focus person, I take his or her attention away from whatever message may be in those tears. Now the focus person is attending to *me*—not the inner teacher—trying to make me feel like a good caregiver: "Thank you for your concern. But please, don't worry about me. I'll be OK. . . ." By engaging the focus person in an interpersonal exchange, I have derailed his or her inner journey. I must remember that for these two hours, I have only one responsibility: to help the focus person devote undivided attention to the voice of true self.

By the same token, if the focus person cracks a good joke, I am not free to laugh long and loud, though a soft smile will do no harm. Once again, behavior that we normally regard as supportive is disruptive and distracting in this setting. By joining the focus person in laughter, I not only call attention to myself—"See, I have a sense of humor too!"—but I may also prevent the focus person from asking a critical inner question: "Am I using my sense of humor to cover up the pain I felt when that question was asked?"

One of the most demanding disciplines of a clearness committee involves eye contact. In our culture, it is generally regarded as impolite *not* to look each other in the eye when we talk. But observe what happens the next time you are in a conversation involving several people. As one person speaks, the listeners send silent signals—smiling and nodding, cocking their heads, furrowing their brows. They give the speaker a steady stream of clues about whether they understand or appreciate whatever he or she is saying.

These clues are meant to be helpful, and so they can be, *if* the speaker's goal is to persuade or connect with other people. But nonverbal clues usually nudge the speaker down a path chosen partly by the listeners, rather than one dictated exclusively by the speaker's inner teacher. As we pick up these signals from others, we often alter what we are saying in the hope of achieving our rhetorical goal.

In a clearness committee, the focus person's goal is to communicate with true self, not with other people. Here nonverbal signals are not just irrelevant; they can easily lead the person down a false path. What committee members think or feel about what a focus person says is of no consequence. The only responses that count are those that come from within the focus person.

So members of a clearness committee try to refrain from nonverbal responses and to listen to the focus person with as much receptive neutrality as they can muster. But most of us find it very hard to achieve this state. So the focus person is encouraged to break eye contact when answering a question or even for the full two hours—to speak with eyes closed or cast down to the floor— in order to avoid seeing the nonverbal signals that committee members may be sending.

At first, the focus person may find it as hard to break eye contact as the committee members find it to withhold nonverbal responses. But after a while, these practices become liberating for everyone. They encourage truthful speaking and receptive listening, drawing us deep into a space that honors and welcomes the soul.

For thirty years, I have used clearness committees to help me make important decisions. As I have listened to people's honest, open questions—and to my inner teacher's response—I have always had the same thought: in this space, I don't need to convince anyone of anything, so there's no one left to fool except myself. In this moment, nothing makes sense except to speak my own truth as clearly as I know how. That simple realization has allowed me to hear, and follow, some inner imperatives that have changed the course of my life.

🎋 Cause for Celebration 🎋

After an hour and a half of questions and responses, the clearness committee enters its final phase. With fifteen minutes remaining, someone asks the focus person if he or she would like members to "mirror back" what they have heard, in addition to asking more questions, or would prefer to continue with the "questions only" rule.

As a focus person, I have always chosen mirroring, because new insights often come to me in that final phase of the process. But because mirroring releases members from the "questions only" rule, it puts us on the edge of a slippery slope where we might start trying to fix, save, advise, or set the focus person straight. So mirroring is protected by clear definitions of what is and is not allowed: it can take three, and only three, forms.

The first involves saying to the focus person, "When you were asked such-and-such a question, you gave such-and-such an answer . . ."—with both the question and the answer being direct quotes, not paraphrases, of what was said. Obviously, if I hold up such a mirror, I think there is something in that question and answer that the focus person needs to see. But I am not allowed to say what that something is, lest I start offering advice. The focus person is free to speak, or not, about the reflection I offer: what matters is not what I see in the focus person's words but what the focus person sees in them as I mirror them back.

The second form of mirroring involves quoting two or three answers the focus person gave to two or three different questions, inviting the person to look at them in relation to one another. By "connecting the dots" in a way that suggests a pattern among the answers, I am coming dangerously close to analyzing the problem and perhaps even proposing a "solution." But again, I am not allowed to describe or even hint at the pattern I think I see. And again, the focus person is free to respond in any way he or she wishes, including saying nothing at all.

The third form of mirroring involves the focus person's body language. I might say to the focus person, "When you were asked about the job offer from the insurance company, you slumped in your chair and spoke in a soft monotone. When you were asked about the offer from the National Park Service, you sat up straight and spoke louder and with inflection."

It is critical that I *describe* rather than *interpret* body language. "You slumped in your chair and spoke in a soft monotone" is a description. "You seemed unenthusiastic, even depressed, as you spoke" is an interpretation. The former allows the focus person to look into the mirror and come to his or her own conclusions about what is there; the latter is a judgment that may create resistance, not receptivity. And my judgment may well be wrong. A posture that says "depressed" to me may reflect deep thoughtfulness in the speaker.

Body language is usually inaudible to the person who "speaks" it. So despite the ever-present slippery slope, mirroring it back in a purely reflective manner can be a great gift to someone who is trying to listen to the inner teacher.

With five minutes remaining in this two-hour process, a committee member needs to say, "It's time for affirmations and celebrations." I have served on many clearness committees, and I have never known these final five minutes to be a false or forced exercise. As the process comes to an end, I almost always realize that I have just seen with my own eyes something amazing and precious: the reality and power of the human soul. I have watched a human being gain important and often unexpected insights from his or her inner teacher. In our kind of world, where the soul is so often shouted down, a chance to welcome it, honor it, and watch it do its work is clearly cause for celebration.

The soul work that goes on in a clearness committee is quiet, subtle, and nearly impossible to put into words. But let the following words from one participant testify to the way the process can give tangible form to the most intangible of emotions:

> The question I have asked myself on so many different levels over the years is "How do I love _____?" The blank space could be filled in with a variety of words—my wife, my children, my parents, my students, my fellow human beings. . . . This has proven to be the most challenging question.
>
> Recently, through my work [in a circle of trust], I gained new insight into this matter. As part of [our time together], we explored and took part in a clearness committee. In this process, I learned a new and most demanding way to listen, a way unencumbered by my own antipathies and judgments. I learned to listen openly for the soul of another, for that which is genuine and sacred.
>
> In a moment of realization, I saw that this was the way I could put love into practice—by listening selflessly with complete attention to another. I could do this at any time with anyone I met. I could simply practice love through listening. Suddenly the most evasive, idealistic notion came softly down to earth.[3]

✿ A Bird in the Hand ✿

We are all shaped by conventional culture. So we all come into a clearness committee carrying a gravitational force that tries to pull our relationships back to fixing, saving, advising, and setting each other straight.

To help people resist this pull, members of a clearness committee are asked to follow behavioral rules so specific that they can seem ludicrous. Do not hand the focus person a tissue if he or she cries; do not laugh aloud if he or she cracks a joke; maintain a neutral expression when speaking and listening; allow the focus person to refrain from making eye contact for two full hours.

When I teach these ground rules, people often say that they feel intimidated by this level of "micromanagement." My response, I confess, is "Good!" When we agree to hold someone's soul in trust, we need to feel the weight of that commitment in order to do the job well. And people who teach others this process need to raise the behavioral bar so high that it will be too embarrassing for anyone to break the rules casually, minimizing the chance that a focus person will be harmed.

But as we raise the bar, we run the risk of turning the clearness committee into a process driven more by law than by the spirit of the law. If we are to make this space safe for the soul, a spirit of hospitality is at least as important as rules that help us act hospitably.

So in addition to teaching the rules, I offer people two clear and simple images that suggest the spirit behind the rules. I offer the first image *before* I teach the rules that have been laid out in this chapter: as members of a clearness committee, we are to create and protect a space to be occupied *only* by the focus person. For two hours, we are to act as if we had no reason for existing except to hold the focus person in a safe space, giving him or her our undivided attention, and guarding the borders of that space against anything that might distract that person.

The rules that guide our behavior are designed to keep us from invading that space, from saying or doing anything that would draw attention toward ourselves. That is why we cannot explain ourselves when the focus person objects to a question or offer comfort when the focus person cries or interpret the focus person's nonverbal speech. Behaviors like these put our needs and agendas into the space, displacing the focus person's soul.

The image of "creating and protecting a space" where we can attend exclusively to the focus person answers almost every question about the conduct of a clearness committee. Should I take notes as the focus person speaks? If note-taking distracts me from attending to the focus person, the answer is no; if note-taking helps me pay attention, the answer is yes. What if the focus person or a member of the committee needs to use the bathroom? The focus person will leave with a brief explanation, and members will maintain silence until he or she returns; a committee member will leave quietly, without explanation, while the process continues and will return to the circle as quietly as he or she left.

There is one more rule that helps us hold safe space for the focus person—the rule of "double confidentiality." Once the committee ends, nothing said in it will ever be repeated to anyone. People who took notes during the meeting must give them to the focus person before they leave. This not only guarantees confidentiality, but it also leaves the focus person with a great gift: a detailed record of what his or her soul was saying when it felt safe enough to tell the truth.

The second part of double confidentiality is as important as the first: committee members are forbidden from approaching the focus person a day, a week, or a year later, saying, "Remember when you said such-and-such? Well, I have a thought to share with you about that." The focus person may seek one of us out for further exploration. But if we were to pursue that person with our feedback or advice, we would violate his or her solitude. Focus persons often say that of all the clearness committee rules, double confidentiality is the one that gives them the most confidence that in this space they can speak their truth freely.

After I have taught the rules, and just before the committee process begins, I offer a second image, an image many have found helpful. For the next two hours, I suggest, we are to hold the soul of the focus person as if we were holding a small bird in the palms of our two hands.

As we do so, we are likely to experience three temptations, and it is important that we resist all of them:

- After a while, our hands may start to close around the bird, wanting to take this creature apart and find out what makes it tick. Resist this temptation: our job is not to analyze but simply to hold in open trust.

- As the time goes by, our arms may begin to tire, and we may find ourselves tempted to lay the bird down: attention flags, the mind wanders, and we are no longer holding the focus person at the center of our awareness. We must resist this temptation too. A bird is light, and a soul is even lighter. If we understand that we are under no obligation to fix, save, advise, or set this person straight, our burden will disappear, and we can hold this soul for two hours without tiring.

- Toward the end of the process—having held the bird openly with the best of intentions—we may find our cupped hands making a subtle but persistent upward motion, encouraging the bird to fly: "Don't you see what you have learned here? Aren't you ready to take off, to act on what you now know?" Resist this temptation too. This bird will fly when it is ready, and we cannot possibly know when that will be.

The success of a clearness committee does not depend on whether the focus person "solves" his or her problem and is ready to act. Life, as everyone knows, does not unfold so neatly. The success of a clearness committee depends simply on whether we have held the focus person safely, for two full hours, in our open hands. When we do, the focus person almost always receives new insights from the inner teacher—and often a revelation or two.

When the clearness committee is finished, we do not need to stop holding the focus person. As the group disbands, the image that often comes to me is that of drawing my open hands into my open heart, where I can continue to hold the focus person in my thoughts, my caring, my prayers.

I have taught this way of "being alone together" to thousands of people over the past thirty years. When the process ends, I always ask, "When was the last time a small group of caring, competent adults held you at the center of their attention for two full hours with nothing on their minds except creating and protecting a space where you could hear your soul speak?" With rare exceptions, I have heard only one answer: "Never in my life have I experienced anything like this."

There are many good ways to be together—life would be quite dreadful if all our interactions were governed by clearness committee rules! Still, it seems a great shame that we spend so much time within easy reach of each other and rarely, if ever, extend this kind of support for each other's inner journey.

But it is never too late. Virginia Shorey was a gifted high school teacher—and an extraordinary human being—who sought and received such support in the final months of her life. A participant in a two-year circle of trust, she learned after the group began that she had incurable cancer; she died before the group ended.

The people in Virginia's circle were companions on her journey, and beneficiaries of her great courage, in part through four clearness committees that Virginia requested and wrote about in her journal:[4]

> Everyone [in these clearness committees] asked me very honest and compassionate questions. I opened myself up to them, my fears, and all the emotions I could not describe. I bared my intentions, my unfinished goals, dreams, and the fear of my life ending so soon, and also my fears for my family. I told them about how I am not through learning and giving yet. I wanted to write a book but now my world was crumbling. My committee did not comfort me. Neither did they fix me. I felt very safe around them. I found strength in their presence. After these [sessions], I began to understand my illness, and even accepted it as a gift. These clearness committees were my allies in getting out of my own jungle.

Shortly before Virginia died, she wrote me to express her gratitude not only for her clearness committees but for her entire circle of trust. I cannot imagine better words with which to close this chapter:

> The reason I'm writing to you is the deep appreciation that I feel in my heart for [this circle]. It has blessed my life so much and has given me all sorts of insights, not only in my teaching but also in my personal and family life.
>
> For one thing, it has given me true courage to respect and honor myself and thus paved new ways to really know myself. It helped me understand the paradoxes of life, especially when I was diagnosed with terminal cancer. It made me aware of my resources. . . .
>
> I've learned to see beyond my senses, to see the spiritual world through silence and meditation, through different eyes. I've learned to appreciate nature like never before, the cycles, the seasons. I've come to the point of seeing that oth-

ers are worthy of my respect, and that I am also worthy of theirs.

Most of all, I learned that we are all a part of a larger community, and hence have tremendously altered my belief system. Because of [this circle], I've learned to conquer my fears and come to know that my resources are limitless. Indeed, I've come to fully understand the courage to live and die and how magnificent it is to know true self!

CHAPTER IX

⚜

On Laughter and Silence
Not-So-Strange Bedfellows

Do not speak unless you can improve upon the silence.
—QUAKER SAYING[1]

*Laughter need not be cut out of anything, since it
improves everything.*
—JAMES THURBER[2]

❧ From Daunted to Doomed ❧

I have found it a bit daunting to try to convey, in print, what it means to speak, listen, and respond in a circle of trust. I hope that the last few chapters have shed some light on the nature of these practices, how they welcome the shy soul and support the journey toward an undivided life. But as I wrote those chapters, I confess that I kept thinking, "You really have to *be there* to get this."

Now, as I set out to write about the role of silence and laughter in a circle of trust, *daunted* does not quite describe how I feel. *Doomed* is closer to the mark! How to write about silence, which is wordless? How to write about the kind of laughter that comes from the right word spoken spontaneously at the right moment? But write I must, because both silence and laughter are vital to creating safe space for the soul.

Silence and laughter may seem like strange bedfellows, but experience reveals that they are not. What, for example, do we call people who can spend hours together in silence without feeling awkward or tense *and* who can use humor to help each other through hard times? We call them, of course, good friends.

It takes good friends to sustain silence and laughter because both make us vulnerable. Silence makes us vulnerable because when we stop making noise, we lose control: who knows what thoughts or feelings might arise if we turned off the television or stopped yammering for a while? Laughter makes us vulnerable because it often comes in response to our flaws and foibles: who knows how foolish we might look when the joke is on us? We can share silence and laughter only when we trust each other—and the more often we share them, the deeper our trust grows.

The soul loves silence because it is shy, and silence helps it feel safe. The soul loves laughter because it seeks truth, and laughter often reveals reality. But above all, the soul loves life, and both silence and laughter are life-giving. Perhaps this is why we have yet another name for people who can share silence and laughter with equal ease: we call them soulmates.

ఞ Laughing With or Laughing At? ঞ

I grew up in a family that laughed a lot and still does. But my parents made sure that we knew the difference between laughing *at* people (a bad thing) and laughing *with* people (a good thing). That distinction came to mind when I learned that *compassion* literally means "feeling with." Compassionate laughter is the kind that emerges as we explore the shared human condition, where comedy is interwoven with tragedy. Laughing *with* each other is a form of compassion, and that is the kind of laughter that goes around a circle of trust.

I facilitated such a circle while I was writing this chapter. Toward the end of our time together, someone reminded us that we would soon be returning to family members and friends who would be asking, "What happened at the retreat?" He said he had found it difficult to share powerful inner experiences with key people in his life and told us about a couple whose marriage was threatened when the wife's inner journey took a direction that the husband did not understand.

Many people nodded in agreement as he spoke, and the mood began to get a bit grim. Then someone reached down and pulled a little red-jacketed book out of his briefcase, saying that he always kept this volume close at hand because it was full of sound counsel for problems large and small.

The book's title, he said, was *Zen Judaism: For You, a Little Enlightenment,* which itself drew a chuckle. But that was nothing compared to the laughter that followed his reading of a "teaching" from the book: "If you practice Zen meditation for long periods of time, you may be criticized by friends and relatives who feel you are shutting them out. Ignore these people."[3]

Our laughter did not mock our friends, our families, or the man who had raised the concern, who laughed as loud at this "Zen teaching" as anyone in the room. We were not laughing *at* anyone; we were laughing *with* each other about our shared condition. Our laughter helped us hold our concern more lightly, increasing the odds that we would deal with it more lovingly.

In fact, once people got home and were asked "What happened?" I imagine that many of them responded by telling this story first, defusing the issue, demystifying the retreat, and opening the way into deeper dialogue. Spiritual gravitas unleavened by humor makes a bread of life that gives us a bellyache.

Laughter can be as helpful as silence in bringing us closer to the sacred. I think, for example, of experiences I have had when young children are present at a family dinner. One of the adults invites us to bow our heads and close our eyes for a moment of silent grace. The adults comply, but two or three of the children cannot resist taking a peek, and the moment their eyes meet, a chain reaction sets in: first the stifled snorts, then the muffled guffaws, then the uncontrollable laughter. In these lovely moments, the laughter of children always strikes me as a form of prayer—easily as valid as what we adults do in silence, a celebration of life's sacredness in which children dwell so deeply.

When we adults stifle laughter to maintain a mask of sobriety, we may well stifle the soul, as one public school teacher learned in a circle of trust. At home, with her family and friends, she was a person who loved to laugh. But the moment she entered the classroom, she put on her professional face, speaking and acting with teacherly reserve, exactly as she had been trained to do.

After many years of teaching, she had begun to burn out. She joined a circle of trust in the hope of renewing her soul—and soon learned that when the "wild animal" within her felt safe enough to appear, it was something of a stand-up comic. Humor, she began to understand, was a vital feature of her true self, and she resolved to try being as true with her students as she was with family and friends.

As she rejoined soul and role, she recovered her joy in teaching. And her students—who now felt safer with a teacher who was more authentic and less forbidding—became more engaged with learning.

嫐 Silent Communion 嫐

My parents' admonition about the two kinds of laughter has parallels when it comes to silence. We can be silent "at" people—as when we give someone "the silent treatment" to convey our disdain or keep a coward's silence when we see injustice inflicted on others. Silence of this sort destroys community and may even make us conspirators with evil.

Or we can be silent "with" people, as in the kind of silence that surrounds reflection, contemplation, and prayer. Silence of this sort—the kind we practice in a circle of trust—is yet another form of human communion. Compassionate silence can help us connect with each other, to touch and be touched by truths that evade all words.

At Pendle Hill, the Quaker community where I lived and worked for eleven years, our lives were so intertwined that people could quickly become attached to each other and just as quickly alienated. But *alienated* is a mild word to describe my relation to one woman who lived there. She was, in my mind, the devil's spawn, sent here directly from the pits of hell to destroy all that is green and good about life on earth.

The people at Pendle Hill gather every morning in a "meeting for worship," forty-five minutes of communal silence, occasionally broken by words spoken spontaneously from the heart. One morning, I arrived late for worship, and the only seat available was next to *her.* Agitated, I came close to turning around and walking out. But I managed somehow to sit down, close my eyes, and start to meditate, slowly forgetting that I was sitting next to a creature from the dark side.

About half an hour later, head still bowed, I opened my eyes and found myself staring at the upturned hand this woman had rested on her knee. There, spotlighted by a shaft of sunlight, I saw the faint but steady throb of an artery in her wrist, the elemental beat of her very human heart. In that moment, I knew beyond words that here was a person just like me, with strengths and weaknesses, hopes and disappointments, joys and despairs. In that moment, my sense of who she was, and of who I was to her, underwent some sort of transformation.

I never became close to this woman. In truth, I never stopped feeling wary of her. But I could no longer demonize her as I had until that silent, sunlit moment. This revelation of her humanity, and this reframing of our relationship, could not have happened, I believe, had I tried to "talk things out" with her. There is a depth of communion in silence that sometimes trumps what we can achieve with words.

Silence in a circle of trust differs from laughter in one important way, besides the fact that it is less noisy. The laughter that deepens our relationships is not a planned practice but a spontaneous response to shared experience. It is not the kind of laughter evoked by a skilled comedian. It is the kind that comes naturally as we spot—and throw the spotlight on—the comedy inherent in everyday life.

But the silence that deepens our relationships must be a conscious practice before it can become a spontaneous response. Why? Because laughter is acceptable in our culture, while silence is not. By creating moments of intentional silence, we smooth the way for spontaneous silence in a culture where the cessation of sound is taken as a sign that something has gone terribly wrong.

Rachel Remen, a physician of body and soul, tells a powerful story about silence as a practice. One of her colleagues attended a conference on Jungian dream analysis where people wrote questions on cards that were passed along to a panel of experts, among whom was the grandson of Carl Jung:

One of these cards told the story of a horrific recurring dream, in which the dreamer was stripped of all human dignity and worth through Nazi atrocities. A member of the panel read the dream out loud. As she listened, my colleague began to formulate a dream interpretation in her head, in anticipation of the panel's response. It was really a "no-brainer," she thought, as her mind busily offered her symbolic explanations for the torture and atrocities described in the dream.

But this was not how the panel responded at all. When the reading of the dream was complete, Jung's grandson looked out over the large audience. "Would you all please rise?" he asked. "We will stand together in a moment of silence in response to this dream." The audience stood for a minute, my colleague impatiently waiting for the discussion she was certain would follow. But when they sat again, the panel went on to the next question.

My colleague simply did not understand this at all, and a few days later she asked one of her teachers, himself a

Jungian analyst, about it. "Ah, Lois," he had said, "there is in life a suffering so unspeakable, a vulnerability so extreme that it goes far beyond words, beyond explanations and even beyond healing. In the face of such suffering all we can do is bear witness so no one need suffer alone."[4]

There are two subtexts to this story that help us understand why "silence with" must be taught and practiced in a circle of trust. First, the silence at the Jungian conference did not arise spontaneously; it was invoked by one of the leaders. Had Jung's grandson not called for silence, the panel might well have slipped into an analytical discussion.

Second, while many people in the room must have understood why silence was the only meaningful response—or else they would have pressed for an interpretation of that dream—Rachel Remen's colleague did not. Trapped in an analytical mind-set, she needed a trusted teacher to explain what had happened and why.

⭑ Silence as Practice ⭑

The sort of silence Rachel Remen writes about is commonplace in circles of trust, sometimes in response to great suffering, sometimes in response to great joy. A silence of this sort conveys not indifference or neglect but reverence and respect. It says to the person who has put his or her truth into the center of the circle, "We will neither invade nor evade the soul truth you have opened to us. We will hold it and you compassionately in the silence."

But helping everyone in the circle become comfortable with silence is a challenge: the fear of silence is driven deep into our psyches. I have heard of studies showing that fifteen seconds of silence is about all the average group can bear. You can do your own research on the subject over the next few weeks. If you are in a group of acquaintances when a moment of silence arrives—a big if in our chatty culture—clock how long it takes someone to speak, even if he or she has nothing to say.

Of course, proof of our fear of silence is also found in our private lives. Most of us work in places filled with noise. But when we leave work and have a chance for some silence, how many of us get into the car and turn on the radio? How many of us turn on the television once we get home? If we free ourselves from these diversions long enough to go for a walk, how many of us take a CD player with a headset? And how many of us are so dependent on a constant stream of chatter that we cannot go anywhere without a cell phone?

One might think that silence would be valued in our religious communities, since they purport to bring us face to face with the sacred mysteries. Yet real silence is rare in most churches I know: more often than not, the air is filled with words or other sounds. I find it especially curious that even on those occasions when the leader calls for a moment of silence—that is, a moment when he or she is not speaking—the "silence" is often accompanied by organ music! And even then, fifteen seconds is about all we get.

But silence is a vital ingredient in a circle of trust, reminding us again of how countercultural these circles are: without silence, we become merely one more group of people crashing through the woods shouting for the soul to come out. All the other key practices that create a circle of trust—using third things, speaking center-to-center, practicing deep listening, and asking honest, open questions—must be couched in and laced with silence if they are to have their best chance of transforming our lives.

To help people become comfortable with silence, the facilitator of a circle of trust must make it a standard practice. By offering early and ongoing opportunities to experience silence as a gift, not a threat, we make it possible for silence to arise spontaneously among us.

For example, in the opening moments of a circle, the facilitator does not begin, as leaders usually do, with greetings, self-introductions, a review of the agenda, and some words of exhortation. Instead, he or she simply says, "Let's take a few minutes in silence to bring ourselves fully to this circle"—and does not break the silence until a full three or four minutes have passed.

As people become more comfortable with starting in silence, they also become more comfortable with silence in midstream, for example, during a dialogue about a third thing. At first, the facilitator may need to remind us to let silence fall between speakers so that everyone will have time to reflect and those who are slow to speak will have a chance to join in. As we see the fruits of these silences, we will need fewer reminders. And in clearness committees, our trust of silence grows deeper still as we see how much the focus person learns in the spaces between the words.

When I worked as a community organizer, I learned that significant change can come from giving people excuses and permission to do things they want to do but are too awkward to do for themselves. The soul wants silence—and when we give people excuses and permission to be silent in a circle of trust, the soul rises to the occasion, often with transforming results.

Why does the soul love silence? The deepest answer I know invokes the mystery of where we came from and where we are headed. At birth, we emerged from the Great Silence into a world that constrains the soul; at death, we return to the Great Silence where the soul is once again free.

Our culture is so fearful of the silence of death that it worships nonstop noise—perhaps as a secular sign of "eternal life"! In the midst of all that noise, small silences can help us become more comfortable with the Great Silence toward which we are all headed. Small silences bring us "little deaths," which, to our surprise, turn out to be deeply fulfilling. For example, as we settle into silence, where our posturing and pushing must cease, we may experience a temporary death of the ego, of that separate sense of self we spend so much time cultivating. But this "little death," instead of frightening us, makes us feel more at peace and more at home.

The Rule of Saint Benedict, that ancient guide to the monastic life, includes the admonition to "keep death before one's eyes daily."[5] As a young man, I found this advice a bit morbid. But the older I get, the more I understand how life-giving this practice can be. As I settle into silence, I draw closer to my own soul, touching a place within me that knows no fear of dying. And the little deaths I experience in silence deepen my appreciation for life—for the light suffusing the room as I write, for the breeze coming in through the window.

So silence brings not only little deaths but also little births—small awakenings to beauty, to vitality, to hope, to life. In silence we may start to intuit that birth and death have much in common. We came from the Great Silence without fear into this world of noise. Perhaps we can return without fear as well, crossing back over knowing that the Great Silence is our first and final home.

❧ Laughter, Silence, and Power ☙

In the next, and final, chapter, I will make the case that welcoming the soul in circles of trust can contribute to a movement for nonviolent social change. I understand how contrarian my thesis is. In a culture that likes to separate inner from outer life, the kinds of ideas explored in this book are commonly regarded as irrelevant to politics.

So I want to lay some groundwork for the next chapter by reflecting on the political significance of laughter and silence. Surely this is an acid test of whether the personal and the political can be joined: of all the things we do in a circle of trust, laughing and being quiet sound like the most apolitical acts of all. But history reveals that laughter and silence have long been used to resist and redirect repressive uses of power.

Satire, for example, is one of the powers of the oppressed most feared by corrupt leaders. When laughter starts to rumble around an unjust regime, it can crack the foundations of power and keep the political seismograph jumping. Hoping to keep the earthquake from gaining momentum, dictators suppress satirists when they can, eliminate them when they cannot, and stay alert for signs of satire arising from underground. Only in a democracy is ridiculing the powerful allowed, and even there, it can help bring them down, as former holders of high office in the United States will attest.

I am blessed to live in a democracy, not a totalitarian state. But the democracy I cherish is constantly threatened by a brand of politics that clothes avarice and the arrogance of power in patriotic and religious garb. There is a classic fable apropos of all this that can teach us much about the political potentials of both laughter and silence: Hans Christian Andersen's tale, "The Emperor's New Suit."[6]

The plot is well known to generations of schoolchildren. Con men posing as tailors come to town and convince the emperor to pay big money for a new suit. To maximize their profits, they make the suit out of thin air and then persuade the emperor that only the ignorant and foolish will be unable to see his "new clothes." Not wishing to be so classified, the emperor agrees to parade through town buck naked—while the townsfolk lining the streets laud his sartorial splendor, not wishing to be so classified any more than he does. The scene provides a classic example of the divided life: emperor and townsfolk alike know the truth inwardly but outwardly live a lie.

The only person with the wit to crack this conspiracy of fools is a little boy who cries out, "The emperor is naked!" The boy's fearful father tries to shut him up. But the innocent outcry has already freed the townsfolk to credit the evidence of their own eyes, setting off a brush fire of recognition that the emperor is utterly bereft of clothing. Amid the throng, this child alone had an undivided life—which, in the words of Thomas Merton, saved all the rest of them from being "madmen or criminals."[7]

The fable does not mention an outburst of laughter among the townspeople. But we are free to imagine that they laughed long and hard—if not out on the streets, then when they got back home. After all, the retelling of this tale has been evoking laughter for a century and a half as people have recognized their own leaders in it, to say nothing of themselves.

Even if these fictional townspeople had been too fearful to laugh in public, they would have made a political statement simply by ceasing to exclaim upon the splendor of the emperor's "new clothes." Had they done no more than fallen into silence and stopped fawning before a lie, it would have caused the political seismograph to jump once again, causing corrupt holders of power to quake.

The message of such silence is simple: "we the people" will no longer conspire in supporting the illusions that help corrupt leaders maintain control. By withholding our cheers and falling into silence, we take a small step toward withdrawing the consent that helps maintain abusive power. We no longer affirm, or pretend to affirm, that the national flags and religious symbols in which corrupt leaders wrap themselves have any meaning—except as an implicit judgment on the duplicity of those leaders.

Of course, the kind of laughter and silence I have been describing are different from the kind we practice in a circle of trust. We laugh *at* corrupt leaders rather than *with* them, and we use silence to dissent from their corruption rather than to express compassion for them.

If my parents were here to suggest that this violates good manners, I would have two excuses to offer—though I am not sure they would be accepted! First, satirical laughter and dissenting silence are nonviolent ways of fomenting social change. People who turn to nonviolence in the face of cruelty and injustice have a much higher claim to good manners than leaders who clothe themselves in piosity and patriotism to justify economic and military violence.

Second, people who share compassionate silence and laughter are readied by those practices to "speak truth to power" in ways that can help heal the body politic. In laughter, we learn to discern the difference between reality and illusion, which serves us well amid the smoke and mirrors of political life. In silence, we remember that someday we will die, which gives us the courage to speak our truth, no matter what the punishment may be.

Courage comes as we understand that no punishment anyone might inflict on us could possibly be worse than the punishment we inflict on ourselves by living a divided life. The divided life ends in the sadness of never having been one's true self. But when we live "divided no more," we always have the last laugh.

That laugh is neither at other people nor with other people—it is at and with ourselves. It comes when we see that our walled-off lives are prisons of our own making, that we defied our own integrity because we feared illusions that now seem laughable. Then we have the last laugh and can act with truth and love in the midst of a violent world. As Mary Oliver has written:

> *I don't know where*
> *such certainty comes from—*
> *the brave flesh*
> *or the theater of the mind—*

but if I had to guess
I would say that only
what the soul is supposed to be
could send us forth
with such cheer.[8]

CHAPTER X

The Third Way

Nonviolence in Everyday Life

Out beyond ideas of wrongdoing and rightdoing,
there is a field. I'll meet you there.
When the soul lies down in that grass,
the world is too full to talk about.
Ideas, language, even the phrase "each other"
doesn't make any sense.

—RUMI[I]

❧ Monday Morning ❧

Early on in my inner journey, I learned about the Monday morning letdown that often follows an uplifting weekend retreat. After soaring for two days, my spirit sank when I got back to work. Faced with the demands of life in the "real world," the inner progress I thought I had made seemed like an illusion, and the new self I thought I had found faded like a mirage.

But I now understand that those letdowns were due only in part to the rigors of the workaday world and my lack of spiritual stamina. The retreats I went on, though well intended, were setups for despair. Shaped by a spirituality that was more about escape than engagement, they gave me a mountaintop experience so rarefied it could not be sustained for long.

A circle of trust does not take us to the mountaintop only to let us down. It puts us on the Möbius strip, where we never leave the ground. Time after time, I have heard participants say, "This is the first retreat I've attended that did not leave me feeling 'high.' Instead, I feel more grounded in myself and more at home in the world."

When we leave a circle of trust, we return to the workplace—or any other arena of life—better able to engage it in life-giving ways. The inner work we have done in that circle reminds us that we are constantly cocreating the world, so we need not be victims of it. Now we go into Monday morning with new understanding of the ancient admonition "I have set before you life and death, blessing and curse: therefore choose life."[2]

Yet when we "choose life," we quickly confront the reality of a culture riddled with violence. By violence I mean more than the physical savagery that gets much of the press. Far more common are those assaults on the human spirit so endemic to our lives that we may not even recognize them as acts of violence.

Violence is done when parents insult children, when teachers demean students, when supervisors treat employees as disposable means to economic ends, when physicians treat patients as objects, when people condemn gays and lesbians "in the name of God," when racists live by the belief that people with a different skin color are less than human. And just as physical violence may lead to bodily death, spiritual violence causes death in other guises—the death of a sense of self, of trust in others, of risk taking on behalf of creativity, of commitment to the common good. If obituaries were written for deaths of this kind, every daily newspaper would be a tome.

Beyond Fight or Flight

By violence I mean *any way we have of violating the identity and integrity of another person.* I find this definition helpful because it reveals the critical connections between violent acts large and small—from dropping bombs on civilians halfway around the world to demeaning a child in a classroom.

Most of us live our lives in the home or classroom or workplace; we play bit parts in the great global drama. But the choices we make in the microarenas of life contribute, for better or for worse, to what happens in the world at large. Even if we do no more than acquiesce to small daily doses of violence, we become desensitized to it, embracing the popular insanity that violence is "only normal" and passively assenting to its dominance.

One of the gifts we are given in a circle of trust is a chance to see how abnormal violence is. Here, under conditions that evoke "the better angels of our nature," we experience our innate capacity to honor, not violate, the identity and integrity of others. And we witness the remarkable things that can happen—within us, between us, and beyond us—as we learn to relate to each other that way.

In a circle of trust, we learn a "third way" to respond to the violence of the world, so called because it gives us an alternative to the ancient animal instinct of "fight or flight."[3] To fight is to meet violence with violence, generating more of the same; to flee is to yield to violence, putting private sanctuary ahead of the common good. The third way is the way of nonviolence, by which I mean *a commitment to act in every situation in ways that honor the soul.*

I have never been in a circle of trust where nonviolence was the focus of discussion, but nonviolence is the tacit curriculum of every such circle I know. As we create a safe space for each other's soul, we discover what it means to live nonviolently, and we develop a vision of how we might live that way in daily life. We begin to see how the principles and practices of the circle could be exported to other parts of our worlds—to the family, the neighborhood, the workplace, and the public arena. Now we understand a simple but significant truth: the third way is not a path of high heroism reserved for the likes of Gandhi and King. It is a path that can, and must, be walked by mortals like you and me.

In fact, walking the third way is much like literal walking: it means taking simple steps, one at a time, steps that honor the soul. Here are three brief examples of what I mean. They are important examples because they involve things that any individual or organization could do. And they all come from the workplace, one of those small arenas of our lives, but an arena where too many people find their identity and their integrity violated.

I know people who, inspired by circles of trust, have found a new way to participate in organizational decision making. Where once they were quick to pick fights by opposing any hint of "wrongheadedness" among their colleagues, now they are more likely to ask honest, open questions about the claims people make—questions that invite dialogue, generate insight, and some-times reveal more unity than people thought they had.

I know supervisors of work groups who, inspired by circles of trust, now begin some of their meetings by inviting a few min-utes of personal storytelling, posing a low-stakes question that allows people to learn a little about each other's lives and helps them feel less like replaceable parts—for example, "What was the best vacation you ever took?" or "How did you earn your first dol-lar outside the home?" or "When you are not at work, what is your idea of a good day?"

I know about a large health care system whose CEO, inspired by a key principle of circles of trust, created safe spaces within the organization where employees can tell the truth with-out penalty. Her organization later won a coveted quality award, largely because of this blame-free zone where doctors and nurses can report their mistakes. "Half the reported incidents lead directly to system improvement," said the CEO—herself a former nurse who "once failed to report her own error in medicating a patient."[4]

If we want to walk the third way, it is important to see how simple such steps can be. It is equally important to see that they are not as simple as they may look! It is daunting to ask honest, open questions in a corporate culture that values speed above thought-fulness or to evoke personal stories in a workplace where people are cautious and self-protective or to invite truth-telling in a field where people habitually dissemble to protect themselves and each other.

A person who walks the third way in settings such as these will likely meet with suspicion, resistance, scorn, or worse—reminding us how pervasive nonphysical violence is. So people who wish to serve as agents of nonviolent change need at least four resources in order to survive and persist: a sound rationale for what they intend to do, a sensible strategy for doing it, a continuing community of support, and inner ground on which to stand.

The core rationale for nonviolence is simple and self-justifying: we act in ways that honor the soul because the soul is worthy of honor. When we act from that motivation, we may or may not change the world. But we will always change ourselves for the better by practicing reverence and respect.

Yet agents of nonviolent change do not lack practical motivation: they know that honoring the soul as an end in itself can strengthen our capacity to do the work of the world well. People who ask honest, open questions in meetings know that when we think together, instead of in isolation or in combat, we are more likely to make good decisions. Supervisors who provide opportunities for team members to learn about each other's lives know that colleagues with personal connections are more productive in general and more resilient in a crisis. CEOs who create blame-free truth-telling zones know that no organization can improve until people feel free to acknowledge and correct their mistakes.

The second resource that agents of nonviolence need is a sensible strategy for change. When people decide to participate in decision making by asking questions instead of arguing, their "strategy" is simply to play this new role with competence and an open heart, modeling new possibilities without attempting to manipulate the outcome. Done this way, a movement toward collaborative decision making may proceed without resistance, because no one notices what is happening! And if the organization starts making better decisions in support of its mission, the practice may multiply.

When supervisors decide that storytelling could strengthen a work group, they do not drop it on people out of the blue. They share their rationale in advance and—if they get enough consent to proceed—they introduce the practice gradually, growing consent as they go. Done carefully and respectfully, with honorable outs for those who are uncomfortable with it, a "bizarre" practice such as storytelling can become the new normalcy, making people feel more visible and more valued.

When CEOs decide to invite risky truth-telling in order to strengthen the corporate mission, they know that the process must begin with some risky truth-telling of their own. It is no accident that the story of that award-winning health care system includes a CEO who publicly acknowledged her own failure to admit a critical mistake. Her strategy was clear and compelling: truth-telling by a leader can legitimate truth-telling at every level.

The third resource vital to agents of nonviolent change is an ongoing community of support. In such a community—in a circle of trust—we do more than learn the principles and practices of nonviolence. We spend time in the company of people who can support our forays into the larger world, people with whom we can share our failures and successes, our hopes and fears, people who can help us find the courage to take the next step.

I know many circles of trust whose original intent was to meet for a year or two. Six, eight, and ten years later, a number of their members still gather regularly. As they went back and forth between the circle and the world, they learned the importance of communal support in sustaining their resolve to live "divided no more."

Finally, agents of nonviolence need inner ground on which to stand. We cannot walk the third way and survive amid "the blizzard of the world" without possessing a place of inner peace, a place that a circle of trust can help us find. But that inner sanctuary is not only for our survival; it is the soulful ground of nonviolent actions that serve others well.

Asking honest, open questions, inviting people to tell their stories, and encouraging organizational truth-telling cannot be mere techniques of management or methods of social engineering. Done from a desire to manipulate and control—and from the fear behind that desire—they are fraudulent and destructive acts. But done vulnerably and with goodwill, such acts can evoke the same qualities in others. We can be peacemakers in our small part of the world only when we are at peace within ourselves.

ᚱ Standing in the Tragic Gap ᚱ

Violence of every shape and form has its roots in the divided life, in that fault line *within* us that cracks open and becomes a divide *between* us. But violence is often more than intra- and interpersonal. Just as the physical violence called war requires massive institutional support, so most forms of nonphysical violence are backed by institutional arrangements that allow it and even encourage it.

From colleges that treat win-lose competition as the best way to make students learn, to medical schools that turn suffering patients into abstract "objects" of study, to religious institutions built on the idea that they alone know the mind of God, to economic institutions that put the rights of capital ahead of the rights of people, to political institutions premised on the notion that might makes right, to cultural institutions that give superiority to people of one race or gender—in all these ways, and more, violence is woven into the very fabric of our collective existence.

The bad news is that violence is found at every level of our lives. The good news is that we can choose nonviolence at every level as well. But what does it mean, in specifics, to act nonviolently? The answer depends on the situation, of course, and a thousand situations might yield a thousand answers. Yet running through all of these answers we will find a single "habit of the heart": to be in the world nonviolently means learning to hold the tension of opposites, trusting that the tension itself will pull our hearts and minds open to a third way of thinking and acting.

In particular, we must learn to hold the tension between the *reality* of the moment and the *possibility* that something better might emerge. In a business meeting, for example, I mean the tension between the fact that we are deadlocked about what to do and the possibility that we might find a solution superior to any of those on the table. In a post–September 11 world, I mean the tension between the fact that we are engaged in the endless cycle of war and the possibility that we might someday live in a world at peace.

Of course, finding a third way beyond our current dilemma may be possible in theory, but it often seems unlikely in life. In a contentious business meeting, a better solution may well exist, but the pressures of ego, time, and the bottom line make it unlikely that we will find it. In a world at war, peace may be our dream, but the grim realities of greed, fear, hatred, and doomsday weaponry quickly turn that dream into a delusion.

The insight at the heart of nonviolence is that we live in a tragic gap—a gap between the way things are and the way we know they might be. It is a gap that never has been and never will be closed. If we want to live nonviolent lives, we must learn to stand in the tragic gap, faithfully holding the tension between reality and possibility in hopes of being opened to a third way.

I harbor no illusions about how hard it is to live in that gap. Though we may try to keep our grip on both reality and hope, we often find the tension too hard to hold—so we let go of one pole and collapse into the other. Sometimes we resign ourselves to things as they are and sink into cynical disengagement. Sometimes we cling to escapist fantasies and float above the fray. Having been drawn to both extremes, I have tried to understand why.

Deep within me there is an instinct even more primitive than "fight or flight," and I do not think it is mine alone. As a species, we are profoundly impatient with tensions of any sort, and we want to resolve every one of them as quickly as we can.

For example, we are in a meeting where a decision must be made. As we talk, it becomes clear that people disagree on the matter, and our frustration grows as we listen to various options. Uncomfortable with holding the tension of conflicting viewpoints and wanting to "get on with it," we call the question, take a vote, and let the majority decide what course we should take.

The tension has been resolved, or so it appears. But by cutting the exploration short, we have deprived ourselves of a chance to find a better way by allowing opposing ideas to enrich and enlarge each other until a new vision emerges. And by letting the majority decide which way we should go, we often drive the tension underground, creating an embittered minority who devote themselves to undermining the decision we thought we had made.

Sometimes our instinct to resolve tension quickly is played out on a much larger stage. When it became clear what had happened on September 11, 2001, the people of the United States were caught in a tension between the violence that had been done to us and what we would do in response. Of course, the outcome was never in doubt. We would respond by wreaking violence on the perpetrators—or on stand-ins who could be made to look like the perpetrators—because that is what nation-states do.

But we had an alternative: we might have held that tension longer, allowing it to open us to a more life-giving response. If we had done so, we might have begun to understand that the terror Americans felt on September 11 is the daily fare of a great many people around the world. That insight might have deepened our capacity for global empathy. That empathy might have helped us become more compassionate and responsible citizens of the international community, altering some of our national policies and practices that contribute to the terror felt daily by people in distant lands. And those actions might have made the world a safer place for everyone, including us.

Had we held the tension longer, we might have been opened to the kinds of actions proposed by William Sloane Coffin—actions that place us in the gap between reality and possibility:

> We will respond, but not in kind. We will not seek to avenge the death of innocent Americans by the death of innocent victims elsewhere, lest we become what we abhor. We refuse to ratchet up the cycle of violence that brings only ever more death, destruction and deprivation. What we will do is build coalitions with other nations. We will share intelligence, freeze assets and engage in forceful extradition of terrorists if internationally sanctioned. [We will] do all in [our] power to see justice done, but by the force of law only, never the law of force.[5]

Instead of holding the tension and being pulled open to options such as these, we allowed ourselves to be caught on the horns of the "fight or flight" dilemma. Since "Americans never turn tail," we fought and, as of this writing, are still fighting. But we do not feel any safer today than we did on September 12, 2001. We have simply acquiesced to fear.

❧ When the Heart Breaks ❧

Why do we hate to hold tension, in matters both large and small? On the surface, the answer seems clear: doing so makes us look uncertain and indecisive. Whether we are in a business meeting or on the global stage, we want to appear powerful, not wimpy. And we want to win. So we call for a vote or send in the troops as quickly as possible.

"Standing in the tragic gap" is unpopular among us because it contradicts the arrogance of power deeply rooted in our egos and our culture. And where does that arrogance come from? The answer, I think, is fear. The more insecure I feel, the more arrogant I tend to become, and the most arrogant people I know are also the most insecure. The arrogant ego does not like it when we hold tension, fearful of losing its status if we lose the battle at hand.

That, at least, is what our fear of tension looks like on the surface. But fear always comes in layers, and can be understood only when we reach its substrate. Ultimately, what drives us to resolve tension as quickly as we possibly can is the fear that if we hold it too long, it will break our hearts.

This bedrock layer of fear is the one that interests me, for at least two reasons. It evokes more sympathy in me, for myself and others, than the ego's fear of looking bad or losing out, which seem whiny and pathetic. And the heart's fear of being broken is not fanciful: holding powerful tensions over time can be, and often is, a heartbreaking experience.

But there are at least two ways to understand what it means to have our hearts broken. One is to imagine the heart broken into shards and scattered about—a feeling most of us know, and a fate we would like to avoid. The other is to imagine the heart broken open into new capacity—a process that is not without pain but one that many of us would welcome. As I stand in the tragic gap between reality and possibility, this small, tight fist of a thing called my heart can break open into greater capacity to hold more of my own and the world's suffering and joy, despair and hope.

If you need testimonials to those options, talk to the parents of a teenage child. Parents often find themselves standing in the tragic gap between their hopes for a child and what is happening in that child's life. If the parents fail to hold that tension, they will go one way or the other, clinging to an idealized fantasy of who "their baby" is or rejecting this "thorn in their side" with bitter cynicism. Both ways of responding are death-dealing for all concerned.

But many parents will testify that by standing in the tragic gap and holding the tension, they not only serve their children well; they themselves become more open, more knowing, more compassionate. E. F. Schumacher painted the picture well:

> Through all our lives we are faced with the task of reconciling opposites which, in logical thought, cannot be reconciled. . . . How can one reconcile the demands of freedom and discipline in education? Countless mothers and teachers, in fact, do it, but no one can write down a solution. They do it by bringing into the situation a force that belongs to a higher level where opposites are transcended—the power of love. . . . Divergent problems, as it were, force us to strain ourselves to a level above ourselves; they demand, and thus provoke the supply of, forces from a higher level, thus bringing love, beauty, goodness and truth into our lives.[6]

If you need a less homey example to prove that holding tension can break the heart open, name anyone who is famous for a personal devotion to truth and justice, love and forgiveness. I cannot think of a person fitting that description who has not spent a lifetime in the tragic gap, torn between the world's reality and a vision of human possibility. That, in brief, is the story of the Dalai Lama, Aung San Suu Kyi, Nelson Mandela, Dorothy Day, Martin Luther King Jr., Rosa Parks, and Thich Nhat Hanh, to name a few. Hearts like theirs have been broken open to a largeness that holds the possibility of a better future for us all.

With these images in mind—images of a million anonymous parents and a few world-famous agents of nonviolent change—I want to revisit the ego's fear that holding tension will make us look weak and keep us from getting results. As proven by the named and the nameless, that fear is not supported by the evidence: the people who achieve the greatest good are those who have the greatest capacity to stand in the tragic gap. Of course, results come more slowly when we hold the tension instead of calling for a vote or sending in the troops. I often hear the argument that there are issues of such practical or moral urgency that holding the tension before we act is not only inefficient but irresponsible.

Sometimes that may be the case—but not always. As with all important questions, how quickly we should act requires discernment. Consider the case of John Woolman (1720–1772), a Quaker who lived in colonial New Jersey. A tailor by trade, Woolman lived among Quaker farmers and businessmen whose affluence depended heavily on slave labor. But Woolman received a revelation from God that slavery was an abomination and that Friends should set their slaves free.

For twenty years, at great personal cost, Woolman devoted himself to sharing this revelation with Quakers, "walking his talk" with every step. When he visited a remote farmhouse to share his revelation, he would fast rather than eat a meal prepared or served by slaves. If he inadvertently benefited from a slave's labor, he would insist on paying that person.

Woolman's message was not always well received by his fellow Quakers, who were, and are, as adept as anyone at living divided lives. In the words of a self-satirizing Quaker quip, "We came to this country to do good and ended up doing well." Woolman's message, if embraced, would require the comfortable Quaker gentry to sacrifice financially.

John Woolman held a terrible tension as he traveled from town to town, farm to farm, meeting to meeting, speaking his truth and standing in the tragic gap between the Quaker vision of "that of God in every person" and the reality of Quaker slaveholding. But hold the tension he did—for two decades—until Quakers reached a consensus that they had to free all of their slaves.

On one level, this is the story of a Christian community that embraced evil and clung to it far too long. Yet the Quakers were the first religious community in this country to free their slaves— and they did so almost eighty years before the Civil War was fought. In 1783, the Quaker community petitioned the Congress of the United States to correct the "complicated evils" and "unrighteous commerce" created by the enslavement of human beings.[7] And from 1827 onward, Quakers played a key role in developing the Underground Railroad.

Quakers took a stand against slavery early in American history partly because one man, John Woolman, was willing to hold the tension between reality and possibility. But it is important to note that the entire Quaker community was also willing to hold that tension until they were opened to a more integral way of being in the world. They refused to succumb to the impulse to resolve the tension prematurely, either by throwing Woolman out or by voting to allow the slavery-approving majority have its way. Instead, they let the tension between reality and possibility break their collective heart open to justice, truth, and love.

There is an old Hasidic tale that tells us how such things happen. The pupil comes to the rebbe and asks, "Why does Torah tell us to 'place these words *upon* your hearts'? Why does it not tell us to place these holy words *in* our hearts?" The rebbe answers, "It is because as we are, our hearts are closed, and we cannot place the holy words in our hearts. So we place them on top of our hearts. And there they stay until, one day, the heart breaks, and the words fall in."[8]

Tension in Circles of Trust

When we sit in a circle of trust, we are given one experience after another in holding the tension of opposites, experiences that slowly break our hearts open to greater capacity. Here are some of the tensions we learn to hold in a circle of trust, a list that simply summarizes topics already explored:

- When we listen to another person's problems, we do not leap to fix or save: we hold the tension to give that person space to hear his or her inner teacher. We learn to neither invade nor evade the reality of each other's lives but rather to find a third way of being present to each other.

- We create a form of community that is mediated by "third things." These poems and stories and works of art allow us to hold challenging issues metaphorically, where they cannot devolve to the pro-or-con choices forced on us by conventional debate.

- Our discourse never involves efforts to persuade or dissuade one another. Instead, each person speaks from his or her center to the center of the circle, where our exploration can take us to a deeper level as we hold the tension involved in weaving a "tapestry of truth."

- Truth in a circle of trust resides neither in some immutable external authority nor in the momentary convictions of each individual. It resides between us, in the tension of the eternal conversation, where the voice of truth we think we are hearing from within can be checked and balanced by the voices of truth others think they are hearing.

In all these ways, and more, a circle of trust moves us toward ways of engaging each other that honor the soul and help us transcend "fight or flight"—ways that open up the possibility of walking the third way in everyday life. Here is another real-world story about how this happens.

Jim was a public school teacher well known among his colleagues for his opposition to high-stakes testing and for his forceful way of arguing for his position on the issue. He joined a two-year circle of trust largely because, after twenty years of teaching, he had reached the point where he was starting to feel burned out. The circle did not change Jim's mind about the merits of high-stakes testing. But it did teach him to listen more deeply to people who disagreed with him about many things—and as he did so, he found his heart breaking open.

Two years after his circle ended, Jim decided to run for election as chair of his school's staff committee in charge of implementing the federal high-stakes testing policy. His opposition to that policy remained strong. But he now saw that the staff needed a safe space where divergent views on the matter could be held with respect—if they were to find a way forward that would not damage the school, each other, or the children. Jim won the election, and under his leadership, the committee helped implement the policy in a way that left virtually everyone concerned feeling honored.

Two features of this story are worth noting. First, Jim nominated himself for this post, revealing how profoundly his self-understanding had been transformed in a circle of trust. Without losing his passionate convictions, he now saw that his primary calling was to hold tensions rather than create them, to build bridges rather than walls. Second, Jim's colleagues elected him to the post, revealing how visible his transformation was to them. The "old" Jim would never have been chosen for such a critical position because his colleagues would not have trusted him to protect a safe space for diverse views and voices.

Before anyone knew that Jim would run for election, someone asked him, "What was the most important thing that happened to you during that two-year circle of trust?" His answer was quick and clear, and it names the inner qualities required to walk the third way: "Through those retreats, I rediscovered a generosity of heart and developed a taste for suffering."

What voice speaks such words? Not the voice of intellect, which talks about facts and theories. Not the voice of emotion, which talks about joy and anger. Not the voice of will, which talks about effort and results. Not the voice of ego, which talks about pride and shame. Only the soul, I think, is able to speak words like those.

The soul is generous: it takes in the needs of the world. The soul is wise: it suffers without shutting down. The soul is hopeful: it engages the world in ways that keep opening our hearts. The soul is creative: it finds a path between realities that might defeat us and fantasies that are mere escapes. All we need to do is to bring down the wall that separates us from our own souls and deprives the world of the soul's regenerative powers.

❧

I thought for a long time before writing the phrase "all we need to do," which makes our task sound simple. For most of my life, bringing down the wall has not been at all simple, and there are days even now when it feels difficult and dangerous to do. But in recent years, I have had more and more days when "unwalling" seems easy, days when I am baffled about why it was once so hard.

When I ask myself why this is so, the answer is in the mirror: I am getting old! With aging, some things get easier, though not everything, of course: I find it more difficult now to get a full night of sleep, to remember what I went upstairs to do, to summon all the synapses required for "multitasking," to start and finish a book . . .

But other things do get easier, and one of them is being myself. Age has robbed me of the energy required to fake it and also of the motivation. I feel less need to try to fool anyone about anything and more need to be here as myself for as much time as I may be granted. The days when I feel this gift of age are days of great blessing, when I can stand in the world like that jack pine on its rocky point, with the simple integrity that comes from being who I am.

Mary Oliver has a poem titled "When Death Comes" that I first read in a circle of trust.[9] It has stayed with me for a decade now, partly because of the way it was opened up for me by that "community of solitudes" and partly because it so clearly speaks to my present condition.

The poem begins by offering image after image of death— "a hungry bear in autumn," "the measle-pox," an "iceberg between the shoulder blades"—images tossed like cold water in the face of any reader who is in denial of death. Then the poem takes a sudden turn—marked by the phrase "And therefore . . ."—followed by a list of the life-giving choices we can make when we embrace our own mortality. It is a list that paints a vivid picture of the undivided life:

> *And therefore I look upon everything*
> *as a brotherhood and a sisterhood,*
> *and I look upon time as no more than an idea,*
> *and I consider eternity as another possibility,*
>
> *and I think of each life as a flower, as common*
> *as a field daisy, and as singular,*
>
> *and each name a comfortable music in the mouth,*
> *tending, as all music does, toward silence,*
>
> *and each body a lion of courage, and something*
> *precious to the earth.*
>
> *When it's over, I want to say: all my life*
> *I was a bride married to amazement.*
> *I was the bridegroom, taking the world into my arms.*

When it's over, I don't want to wonder
if I have made of my life something particular, and real.
I don't want to find myself sighing and frightened,
or full of argument.

I don't want to end up simply having visited this world.

As we embrace the simple fact of our mortality, we also embrace true self. Knowing with new clarity that the gift of life is ours only for a while, we choose to live "divided no more" simply because it would be foolish not to. As we live into that choice, we see with new clarity that all the life around us is "something precious to the earth," and we find more and more ways to honor the soul in ourselves and in every mortal creature.

Notes

Gratitudes

1. For information about these opportunities, go to http://www. teacherformation.org and click on the section for readers of *A Hidden Wholeness*.

2. For further information on the Fetzer Institute, go to http:// www.fetzer.org.

3. For further information on the Center for Formation in the Community College, go to http://www.league.org/league/projects/formation/index.htm.

4. For further information on the work of the Accreditation Commission for Graduate Medical Education, go to http://www.acgme.org and click on "Award Program."

5. D. M. Thomas, "Stone," in John Wain, ed., *Anthology of Contemporary Poetry: Post-War to the Present* (London: Hutchinson, 1979), p. 27.

Prelude

1. Leonard Cohen, "The Future" © 1992 by Sony Music Entertainment, Inc.

Chapter I, Images of Integrity: Living "Divided No More"

1. Douglas Wood, *Fawn Island* (Minneapolis: University of Minnesota Press, 2001), pp. 3–4.

2. Thomas Merton, "Hagia Sophia," in Thomas P. McDonnell, ed., *A Thomas Merton Reader* (New York: Image/Doubleday, 1974, 1989), p. 506.

3. U.S. Department of Agriculture, *A Changing Forest* (Washington, D.C.: Government Printing Office, 2001).

4. Rumi, "Forget Your Life," in Stephen Mitchell, ed., *The Enlightened Heart* (New York: HarperCollins, 1989), p. 56.

5. Sam Waksal, interview with Steve Kroft, *60 Minutes,* CBS News, Oct. 6, 2003. See http://www.cbsnews.com/stories/2003/10/02/60minutes/main576328.shtml.

6. Noah Porter, ed., *Webster's Revised Unabridged Dictionary* (Springfield, Mass.: Merriam, 1913), p. 774.

7. John Middleton Murry, quoted in M. C. Richards, *Centering* (Middleton, Conn.: Wesleyan University Press, 1989), epigraph.

8. "Persons of the Year," *Time,* Dec. 30, 2002–Jan. 6, 2003, pp. 30 ff.

9. Ibid., p. 33.

10. Ibid.

11. For more information about the program for public school educators, go to http://www.teacherformation.org.

12. For more information about the expanded program, go to http://www.teacherformation.org and click on the section for readers of *A Hidden Wholeness.*

Chapter II, Across the Great Divide: Rejoining Soul and Role

1. Rainer Maria Rilke, in Stephen Mitchell, ed., *The Selected Poetry of Rainer Maria Rilke* (New York: Vintage Books, 1984), p. 261.

2. Rumi, "Someone Digging in the Ground," in Coleman Barks and John Moyne, trans., *The Essential Rumi* (San Francisco: HarperSanFrancisco, 1995), p. 107.

3. C. S. Lewis, *The Chronicles of Narnia* (New York: HarperCollins, 1994).

4. Vaclav Havel, *The Power of the Powerless* (New York: Sharpe, 1985), p. 42. The Velvet Revolution refers to the bloodless overthrow of the Communist government of Czechoslovakia in 1989.

5. Rilke, *Selected Poetry,* p. 261.

6. I am not the first to use the phrase "circle of trust," though, as far as I know, the meaning I attach to it is my own. Search the Web for the phrase, and you find "circles of trust" being used for purposes that range from improving the economic status of the poor in developing nations (http://www.lightlink.com/cdb-l/archives/12.94-3.96/1303.html) to verifying individual identities in the anonymity of cyberspace (http://www.sciam.com/2000/0800issue/0800cyber.html). And in the movie *Meet the Parents,* Robert De Niro's character refers to a "circle of trust" with great sardonic effect!

7. See http://www.orgdct.com/more_on_t-groups.htm.

8. C. S. Lewis, op. cit.

9. I am grateful to Johnny Lewis for giving me permission to use his words.

10. Diana Chapman Walsh, "Cultivating Inner Resources for Leadership," in Frances Hesselbein, ed., *The Organization of the Future* (San Francisco: Jossey-Bass, 1997), p. 300.

CHAPTER III, EXPLORATIONS IN TRUE SELF:
INTIMATIONS OF THE SOUL

1. Mary Oliver, "Maybe," in Robert Bly, ed., *The Soul Is Here for Its Own Joy: Sacred Poems from Many Cultures* (Hopewell, N.J.: Ecco Press, 1995), p. 15.

2. Thomas Merton, *The Inner Experience* (San Francisco: HarperSanFrancisco, 2003), p. 4.

3. Mary Oliver, "Low Tide," *Amicus Journal,* Winter 2001, p. 34.

4. A fuller account of my experience with depression is found in Chapter IV of my book *Let Your Life Speak* (San Francisco: Jossey-Bass, 2000).

5. Erica Goode, "Making Sense of Depression," *Oregonian,* Feb. 9, 2000, p. B1. See also Randolph M. Nesse, "Is Depression an Adaptation?" *Archives of General Psychiatry,* 2000, *57,* 14–20.

6. Robert Pinsky, trans., *The Inferno of Dante* (New York: Noonday Press, 1994), I:1–7.

7. Human Rights Campaign Foundation, *Finally Free: Personal Stories:*

How Love and Self-Acceptance Saved Us from "Ex-Gay" Ministries (Washington, D.C.: Human Rights Campaign Foundation, 2000), p. 2.

8. Mark Bowden, "Tales of the Tyrant," *Atlantic Monthly,* May 2002, p. 40.

9. W. H. Auden, "Under Which Lyre," in *Collected Poems of W. H. Auden* (London: Faber & Faber, 1946).

10. The Möbius strip was discovered in 1858 by German mathematician and astronomer August Ferdinand Möbius. The mathematical equation that produces the shape is known as the Möbius transformation or bilinear transformation.

11. T. S. Eliot, "Four Quartets: Little Gidding," in *The Complete Poems and Plays, 1909–1950* (New York: Harcourt, 1952), p. 145.

CHAPTER IV, BEING ALONE TOGETHER:
A COMMUNITY OF SOLITUDES

1. Robert Bly, *The Morning Glory: Prose Poems* (New York: Harper-Collins, 1975), epigraph.

2. The idea that "Whose am I?" is as important a question as "Who am I?" is one I got in conversation with the late Douglas Steere, a Quaker philosopher and writer who taught at Haverford College.

3. Dietrich Bonhoeffer, *Life Together* (New York, HarperCollins, 1954), p. 78.

4. See Igumen Chariton of Valamo, *The Art of Prayer: An Orthodox Anthology* (London: Faber & Faber, 1997), pp. 110, 183.

5. *Fellowship,* Nov.-Dec. 1997, p. 23, citing Tissa Balasuriya, *Mary and Human Liberation* (Harrisburg, Pa.: Trinity Press International, 1997).

6. Rumi, "I Have Such a Teacher," in Bly, *Soul Is Here,* p. 160.

7. Rainer Maria Rilke, *Letters to a Young Poet,* trans. M. D. Herter (New York: Norton, 1993), p. 59.

8. Nikos Kazantzakis, *Zorba the Greek* (New York: Simon & Schuster, 1952), pp. 120–121.

9. I used this story in my book *The Courage to Teach* (San Francisco:

Jossey-Bass, 1998), pp. 59–60. I retell it here from a different angle and for a different purpose.

Chapter V, Preparing for the Journey: Creating Circles of Trust

1. Stuart Brubridge, "Quakers in Norfolk and Norwich," Quaker Faith and Practice, sec. 24.56. See http://www.qnorvic.com/quaker/qfp/QF&P_24.html.

2. Joseph Heller, *Catch-22* (New York: Simon & Schuster, 1996). For a definition of *catch-22,* see http://www.angelfire.com/ca6/uselessfacts/words/002.html.

3. For further information about retreats and resources related to circles of trust, go to http://www.teacherformation.org and click on the section for readers of *A Hidden Wholeness.*

4. The Courage to Teach program of the Center for Teacher Formation makes use of seasonal metaphors.
See http://www.teacherformation.org.

5. See Chapter IV, note 2.

6. Thomas Merton, "The General Dance," in McDonnell, *Thomas Merton Reader,* pp. 500–505.

7. For a fuller, more personal meditation on the seasonal metaphors, see Chapter VI of my book *Let Your Life Speak.*

8. Derek Wolcott, "Love After Love," in *Collected Poems, 1948–1984* (New York: Noonday Press, 1987), p. 328.

Chapter VI, The Truth Told Slant: The Power of Metaphor

1. "Poem 1129," *The Complete Poems of Emily Dickinson,* http://members.aol.com/GivenRandy/r_emily.htm.

2. May Sarton, "Now I Become Myself," in *Collected Poems, 1930–1973* (New York: Norton, 1974), p. 156.

3. Emily Dickinson, loc. cit.

4. T. S. Eliot, Nobel Prize acceptance speech, 1948.

5. Some important matters facilitators need to consider when they use

third things are not addressed in this chapter, since this book was not designed as a facilitation handbook. A few examples of such matters, briefly noted: Use third things from various wisdom traditions to make sure no one feels excluded. The first time you use a third thing, it should be from a tradition that is unlikely to have adherents in the circle (such as Taoism) so that no one has a position to defend; then, when you use a story from a tradition whose adherents are present (such as Christianity or Judaism), you can invite participants to approach the story as openly and inquisitively as they approached the first one. Use poems or stories that are relatively brief and transparent so that people do not waste time trying to understand the text that they could better use trying to understand themselves. Use only third things that both speak to you as a person and you find teachable as a facilitator. Deeper insight into these and other important details of leadership for circles of trust can be gained through the programs described at http://www.teacherformation.org.

6. "The Woodcarver," in Thomas Merton, ed., *The Way of Chuang Tzu* (New York: New Directions, 1965), pp. 110–111. I first wrote about the "The Woodcarver" in Chapter 4 of my book *The Active Life* (San Francisco: Jossey-Bass, 1991).

7. Robert Pirsig, *Zen and the Art of Motorcycle Maintenance* (New York: Morrow, 1974), makes it clear why I included a mechanic in this list!

CHAPTER VII, DEEP SPEAKS TO DEEP: LEARNING TO SPEAK AND LISTEN

1. William Stafford, "A Ritual to Read to Each Other," in *The Way It Is: New and Selected Poems* (Saint Paul, Minn.: Graywolf Press, 1998), p. 75.

2. Nelle Morton, *The Journey Is Home* (Boston: Beacon Press, 1985), pp. 55–56.

3. Barry Lopez, *Crossing Open Ground* (New York: Scribner, 1988), p. 69.

4. I explore this "good case–bad case" method in my book *The Courage to Teach*, pp. 66–73. Since writing those pages, I have learned that working with the "bad case" is made easier by following the basic rule of the "clearness committee" (asking honest, open questions

about the case) and honoring the spirit behind that rule, as explained in Chapter VIII of this book. See also Richard Ackerman, *The Wounded Leader* (San Francisco: Jossey-Bass, 2002), pp. 145–147, for guidance on using what he calls "case stories."

5. Martin Buber, *Tales of the Hasidim: Early Masters* (New York: Schocken Books, 1974), pp. v–vi.

6. By "passion" I do not mean shouting and waving one's hands. I mean a soul-deep sensibility that can range from joy to suffering—from the passion felt by lovers to "the passion of Christ"—an understanding that restores the root meaning of the word. That root also gives rise to *patience,* a virtue required by "the eternal conversation"!

CHAPTER VIII, LIVING THE QUESTIONS: EXPERIMENTS WITH TRUTH

1. Rilke, *Letters to a Young Poet,* p. 35.

2. Setting up clearness committees in a circle of trust sometimes involves a little math. A circle of seven people or less can serve as a "committee of the whole" for one of its members. But circles of larger size need to have enough volunteers as focus persons so that everyone can be on a committee without any committee being too large or too small; for example, in a circle of seventeen, three volunteers are needed, and in a circle of twenty-four, four volunteers are needed. When clearness committees are formed in the context of a larger circle, committee members are assigned by the facilitator (rather than chosen by the focus person, as they are when a committee is formed apart from such a circle). Before making the assignments, the facilitator asks each focus person for two lists of names: people that he or she would especially like to have on the committee and people that he or she would not want to have on the committee. The facilitator assigns as many from the first list as possible and guarantees not to assign any from the second list.

3. I am grateful to Jack Petrash for giving me permission to use his words.

4. I am grateful to the late Virginia Shorey, a brave and inspiring woman, who sent me these words and gave me permission to use them. And I am grateful to her husband, Roscoe Shorey, who gave me permission to use her name here.

CHAPTER IX, ON LAUGHTER AND SILENCE:
NOT-SO-STRANGE BEDFELLOWS

1. I first heard this saying from Quakers, and have always imagined that it originated with them. But in searching for it on the Web, I see it is attributed to a variety of sources—including Buddhism, an anonymous monk, and Mark Twain—so I probably would have been wise to stay silent regarding its source!

2. Helen Thurber and Edward Weeks, eds., *Selected Letters of James Thurber* (Boston: Atlantic/Little, Brown, 1981).

3. David M. Bader, *Zen Judaism: For You, a Little Enlightenment* (New York: Harmony Books, 2002), p. 75.

4. Rachel Remen, *My Grandfather's Blessings* (New York: Riverhead Books, 2000), pp. 104–105.

5. Boniface Verheyen, trans., *The Holy Rule of St. Benedict* (Atchison, Kans.: Saint Benedict's Abbey, 1949), ch. 4, no. 47.

6. "The Emperor's New Suit," in Lily Owens, ed., *Complete Hans Christian Andersen Fairy Tales* (New York: Gramercy, 1993), p. 438.

7. Thomas Merton, *Raids on the Unspeakable* (New York: New Directions, 1966), p. 62.

8. Mary Oliver, "Walking to Oak-Head Pond, and Thinking of the Ponds I Will Visit in the Next Days and Weeks," in *What Do We Know?* (Cambridge, Mass.: Da Capo Press, 2002), p. 54.

CHAPTER X, THE THIRD WAY:
NONVIOLENCE IN EVERYDAY LIFE

1. Rumi, "Quatrain 158," in John Moyne and Coleman Barks, trans., *Open Secret: Versions of Rumi* (Santa Cruz, Calif.: Threshold Books, 1984), p. 36.

2. Deuteronomy 30:19.

3. I first heard the phrase "the third way" during the Vietnam War, in connection with a Buddhist effort to bring the warring parties together. I saw the phrase most recently in Walter Wink, "Nonviolent Resistance: The Third Way," an occasional paper from the Wider Quaker Fellowship, reprinted from the Winter 2002 issue of *Yes! A Journal of Positive Futures,* where it appeared under the title "Can Love Save the World?"

4. David S. Broder, "Promising Health Care Reform Passes Almost Unnoticed," *Washington Post,* Apr. 9, 2003.

5. William Sloane Coffin, "Despair Is Not an Option," *Nation,* Jan. 12, 2004.

6. E. F. Schumacher, *Small Is Beautiful: Economics as if People Mattered* (New York: HarperCollins, 1973), pp. 97–98.

7. See http://www.rootsweb.com/~quakers/petition.htm.

8. I heard this Hasidic tale from philosopher and writer Jacob Needleman, who kindly put it in writing for me so I could recount it correctly.

9. Mary Oliver, "When Death Comes," in *New and Selected Poems* (Boston: Beacon Press, 1992), pp. 10–11.

The Author

PARKER J. PALMER is founder and senior partner of the national Center for Courage & Renewal (www.CourageRenewal.org), which oversees "Courage to Teach," "Courage to Lead" and "Circle of Trust"® programs for people in the serving professions (including education, medicine, ministry, law, and philanthropy), as well as people in other walks of life. For fifteen years, he served as senior associate of the American Association of Higher Education. He now serves as senior advisor to the Fetzer Institute.

A writer, traveling teacher, and activist, Dr. Palmer focuses on issues in education, community, leadership, spirituality, and social change. His work has spoken to people in many sectors of our society, including public schools, college and universities, religious institutions, corporations, foundations, and grassroots organizations.

He has published a dozen poems, some two hundred essays, and seven books, including several best-selling and award-winning titles: *A Hidden Wholeness, Let Your Life Speak, The Courage to Teach, The Active Life, To Know as We Are Known, The Company of Strangers,* and *The Promise of Paradox.*

Dr. Palmer's work has been recognized with ten honorary doctorates, two Distinguished Achievement Awards from the

National Educational Press Association, an Award of Excellence from the Associated Church Press, and major grants from the Danforth Foundation, the Lilly Endowment, and the Fetzer Institute.

In 1993, he won the national award of the Council of Independent Colleges for Outstanding Contributions to Higher Education.

In 1998, The Leadership Project, a national survey of 10,000 administrators and faculty, named Dr. Palmer as one of the thirty "most influential senior leaders" in higher education and one of the ten key "agenda-setters" of the past decade, stating, "He has inspired a generation of teachers and reformers with evocative visions of community, knowing, and spiritual wholeness."

In 2001, Carleton College gave Dr. Palmer the Distinguished Alumni Achievement Award.

In 2002, the Accreditation Council for Graduate Medical Education created the "Parker J. Palmer Courage to Teach Award," given annually to the directors of ten medical residency programs that exemplify patient-centered professionalism in medical education.

In 2003, the American College Personnel Association named Dr. Palmer a "Diamond Honoree" for outstanding contributions to the field of student affairs.

In 2005, Jossey-Bass published *Living the Questions: Essays Inspired by the Work and Life of Parker J. Palmer*, written by notable practitioners in a variety of fields including medicine, law, philanthropy, politics, economic development, and K–12 and higher education.

Parker J. Palmer received the Ph.D. in sociology from the University of California at Berkeley. A member of the Religious Society of Friends (Quaker), he lives with his wife, Sharon Palmer, in Madison, Wisconsin.

Index

Index

BRINGING THE BOOK TO LIFE

A Reader's and Group Leader's Guide to
Exploring the Themes in
A Hidden Wholeness

❧

CARYL HURTIG CASBON
AND
SALLY Z. HARE

The authors and Parker J. Palmer are grateful to the Lilly Endowment, Inc., for its generous support of the production of this leader's guide and of the *Circles of Trust* DVD.

PART I:
LEADING FROM WITHIN

As two people who have facilitated Circle of Trust® retreats for more than a decade, we were delighted when our friend and colleague Parker Palmer invited us to prepare a guide for people who would like to lead a group exploration of *A Hidden Wholeness,* using the principles and practices described in the book. We know the power of this process and are glad to share some of what we know with you. We hope that this guide will give you a way to bring the content and the spirit of the book alive in a study group under your leadership—which may in turn help participants carry the experience into other parts of their lives.

We want to be clear about two things as we get under way. First, the process proposed here is not a typical "book study group." As your group studies *A Hidden Wholeness* and comes to terms with its ideas through a process shaped by those ideas, the participants will be studying themselves! This book is about deciding to live "divided no more." So the journey you will lead is not an academic quest in response to the question "What's that book all about and what do I think about it?" It is a personal inquiry animated by the question "What am *I* all about and what do I think about that?" The sensibilities and skills required to lead people on a soul-searching journey are different from those required to lead people in searching out a text.

The second thing we want to be clear about is equally important. Reading this guide and leading a study group based on the book's principles will, we hope, add to your leadership repertoire. But it will *not* prepare you to facilitate in-depth retreats based on the Circle of Trust® approach used by the Center for Courage & Renewal, a nonprofit organization developed in collaboration with Parker Palmer. Having promised participants "safe space for the soul" in its programs, the Center takes seriously the ethical responsibility that comes with the facilitator role and exercises great care in choosing and preparing people to facilitate its offerings. The skill and sensibility of the facilitator is the Center's primary means of "quality control" in its Circle of Trust® approach; only facilitators prepared by the Center can use the capitalized and registered version of that name. (More on this topic will be found on pages 75–78 in *A Hidden Wholeness*.)

If you are interested in formal facilitation, please contact the Center to learn more about the facilitator preparation program. Visit the Web site of the Center for Courage & Renewal at http://www.CourageRenewal.org to learn more about the growing Courage community and the many manifestations of this work around the country.

People who lead circles of trust in any form must understand that the leader's first task is to do his or her own inner work, integrating the principles and practices described in *A Hidden Wholeness* into their own lives before offering them to others. In that spirit, we invite you to assess your *own* readiness to lead this book study group by reflecting on the questions we pose here, perhaps discussing them with a trusted friend. Ask yourself, Am I ready to serve from a calm presence and strong sense of self amid the complexities of a group?

People know instinctively whether a leader has the capacity to work with challenging personalities, conflict, power struggles, and diversity in its many guises. Faced with such demands, a leader must be able to "stand outside" the process enough to read the group calmly, not get his or her ego involved, and deal with the group's evolving needs. But there is an important paradox here. Even while

---

About Circles of Trust®

In *A Hidden Wholeness,* Parker Palmer uses the generic phrase "circle of trust" to describe a range of activities, from a setting where two or three people are gathered to a book study or support group to a formal retreat. The registered name Circle of Trust® is used to designate the approach used by facilitators who have been selected and prepared by the Center for Courage & Renewal to lead its programs.

About the Center for Courage & Renewal

Located on Bainbridge Island, Washington, the Center for Courage & Renewal has prepared over 175 facilitators in thirty states and fifty cities as well as several in Canada and Australia; has supported affiliate programs in Dallas–Fort Worth, Boston, and Washington State; and has served over twenty-five thousand people in retreat settings since 1997. At the Center's Web site (http://www.CourageRenewal.org), you will find contact information for our facilitators and descriptions of current offerings and can sign up for our electronic newsletter as well as download articles and podcasts. We welcome your interest and invite you to learn more about our work and our community.

"standing outside," the leader of a circle of trust must be involved in it, lest participants feel that the leader is keeping the process at arm's length, asking participants to take risks of vulnerability that the leader is unwilling to take.

But even as leaders bring their own lives into the circle, they must have the restraint and the professionalism not to "breathe up all the oxygen in the room." In particular, this kind of leadership requires us to work on our own wounds outside the group—for as we have learned, pain that is not transformed is pain that is transmitted. We cannot lead well if we use the circle to work with our own shadow or, worse, unconsciously act our shadow out on the participants. Among Courage facilitators, the rule is simple: "We need this work as much as the people we are serving. But if we need it too much to lead well, we won't be serving them." So ask yourself, Do I have what it takes to do my own inner work outside of this process so that I am able both to participate in it and to lead it well?

At the heart of all that we do as Courage facilitators is our belief that "we teach who we are." Those of us who lead such circles know that they are safe only in the hands of people who are grounded in their own integrity, who are in touch with and guided by their souls. As a group leader, your identity and integrity are the most important qualities you have to offer. Embodiment is where everything begins: your presence and your clarity about the ground on which you stand set the tone for what is possible in a circle of trust.

The choice of inner practices to find this ground is, of course, individual. However, a regular commitment to slowing down, to solitude and silence, to some form of reflection through journaling, or to spending time in nature are examples of practices that help keep that "rope to the barn" (pp. 1–2) secure. Ask yourself, What practices work best for me in support of my own inner work, and how can I stay faithful to them?

Finally, those of us who lead have learned that it is vital to have trusted colleagues and friends who can challenge us and help create these circles for others: it is wise to not "go it alone." We encourage you to choose a partner for creating and leading this book group. Circles of trust are meant to help create community, so they are best planned and held in community with others who share that commitment, who will speak truth, share feedback, and keep us on track through mutual discernment. Besides, it's more fun that way! So we ask you to ask yourself one more question: With whom would I like to partner in creating this book group?

If and when you feel ready to proceed, Part II of this guide offers chapter-by-chapter suggestions for group reflection and discussion. In Part III, you will find stories from people who have experienced the circle of trust process and have "taken it home" in various ways, internalizing its principles and practices and integrating them into their family lives, workplaces, and communities.

We thank you for sharing our commitment to the disciplines and goals of this work. And we wish you a meaningful, trustworthy, and joyful journey as you lead your book study group!

PART II:
A CHAPTER-BY-CHAPTER GUIDE
TO *A HIDDEN WHOLENESS*

A Hidden Wholeness is about taking a journey toward an undivided life supported by a circle of trust, a "community of solitudes" where people come together in a way that gives every participant a chance to attend to the inner teacher and learn from one another. What follows are chapter-by-chapter recommendations for designing and leading a book study group in the manner of circles of trust. Our recommendations are based on the assumption that such a group might meet for an hour or two a week over ten to twelve weeks; you may want to adjust our suggestions to fit your group and your leadership style.

It is critical that everyone who joins your group understands clearly what is going to happen and chooses to be there on that basis. This is not a typical book study group! In the spirit of the book being studied, people will be invited to do "soul work" here, work that will be resisted or undermined by participants who did not understand what they were getting into. So as you extend invitations to potential participants, be transparent about how this differs from other book groups they may have known. As we said earlier, the key difference is that people in this group will be studying themselves as well as the book, and they need to be clear about that in advance. If they are not, anticipate trouble!

Before we go through the book chapter by chapter, let's consider how creating a circle of trust group will be different from the traditional book group, including the role of the leader:

1. **In this group, the leader does not teach the book as a traditional book group leader might.** The leader's role is to create safe space where participants can move back and forth between ideas and experience, exploring the book's themes in a way that becomes an exploration of their own lives. You will not be "covering" the material in each chapter but establishing the condi-

tions in which participants use *A Hidden Wholeness* to listen to themselves, to their own inner wisdom, through the use of appropriate third things, careful structure, and open and honest questions. This is not a place to ask, "What do you think the author meant?" about this or that. (You might want to reread pages 93–94, where Palmer describes his response to a participant who was an expert on the poetry of May Sarton.)

2. **In this group, the leader is also a participant.** This means that he or she does not stand outside of the process as its "manager" but is engaging in self-searching with the rest of the group. But at the same time, he or she must always be aware of the leader's responsibility and be willing to fulfill it. The group must feel the safety that comes from knowing that the leader is paying close attention to the participants and their comments (which includes not letting one or two people dominate), as well as to the agenda, schedule, boundaries, and goals of the exploration. The group must have a sense of generous, unhurried time so that the process feels spacious rather than jam-packed with a long to-do list (see pp. 84–86).

3. **The "third thing" in this circle is the material in *A Hidden Wholeness*.** Intentionality in a circle of trust is achieved by focusing on an important topic, and as Palmer writes, the shy soul responds best to an indirect approach through the use of a *third thing* (see pp. 91–94). In this guide, we suggest ways to use some of the ideas, poems, and stories in the book as third things for your sessions.

4. **The conversation in this circle is not about yes-or-no or right-or-wrong answers.** In a traditional book group, questions are often along the lines of "Do you agree with the author on *X*?" Here we use open and honest questions to which no one has the "correct" answer, and we use expressive rather than instrumental speech (see pp. 118–119). Rather than agreeing or disagreeing

with the book or with each other, participants are invited to let the questions and materials evoke their own experience, their own lives. In the pages that follow, we suggest questions that can help you create and hold this kind of self-learning space.

5. **The group's path through the book need not be a linear one.** You might want to revisit or spend more time on certain chapters in order to draw your group deeper into some of its insights. You may choose to introduce parts of the book nonsequentially; for example, in the early meetings, you could bring in some of the ideas from Chapter V, where the role of the leader and the kind of space needed for a circle of trust are articulated, so that your participants can understand and support you in creating and holding the circle.

6. **The leader's understanding of the principles and practices of the circle of trust is a critical factor in creating one.** So in addition to reading the book with care and absorbing it, take time to watch the DVD included with it (see the accompanying box). In the pages that follow, we recommend particular sections of the DVD that you can integrate into almost every meeting to enliven and deepen the group's focus, so it will help if you are familiar with the whole scope of the DVD as you proceed with this guide.

7. **In this book group, as in life, we lead who we are.** We hope that the design suggestions that follow will not only support your group leadership but will also evoke your own ideas for your group. While there are some clear and important guidelines for leading this process in a way that protects the integrity of the circle and of each individual in it, within those boundaries you must adapt in ways that are authentic to and for you. Your authority as leader—which is critical in creating safe space—comes in part from the group's perception that what you are doing with it is integral to who you are.

Circles of Trust DVD:
The Work of Parker Palmer

Included with this edition of *A Hidden Wholeness* is a DVD titled *Circles of Trust: The Work of Parker Palmer,* in which Palmer is interviewed about many of the themes in the book. This is a valuable companion to this book group process and useful when introducing this work to others.

One more thing before we begin: "less is more" when it comes to creating a circle of trust. In that spirit, we suggest the following simple four-step structure for each session of your book group, steps we fill out in more detail in the chapter-by chapter design proposals that follow:

1. **Welcome, Opening Reading, and Brief Silent Reflection.** The welcome is important in setting the tone of hospitality. A short reading or DVD selection followed by a minute or two of silence will help participants come into the space. Though silence is a scarce commodity in our culture, and it makes many people nervous, it is an important ingredient for self-reflection and a staple in circles of trust.

2. **Reading of the Touchstones.** In a moment, we will offer a set of "touchstones" that will help you define clear boundaries for the circle, the kinds of boundaries that help create safe space for the soul.

3. **Open and Voluntary Group Sharing.** An important part of each session is "being alone together," having the opportunity to listen and be listened to, and hearing yourself speak your thoughts into the circle of trust.

4. **Closing Circle.** We end our circles with a "grace note": participants settle into silence and then speak briefly about insights they have gained in the time together or feelings they have as

the time comes to an end. A closing reading or a segment of the DVD can also be used during this time.

Opening Session: Prelude: The Blizzard of the World (pp. 1–2)

Welcome and Reflection

The initial session is especially important in setting the culture and tone of the group. The practices that create circles of trust and make them safe for the soul are often countercultural, so you will be asking participants to set aside ways they would ordinarily behave in relation to one another.

As you welcome the group for the first time, we suggest being transparent (as you were when you first extended the invitation to join the book group) about how this group differs from traditional book groups. Before the group meets, ask people to bring personal journals to every session. Now underscore the fact that they will be using their journals primarily for reflecting on their own inner process, rather than focusing on what you or other participants say. (You may want to read the section on taking notes on one's own words, on page 93, before the opening reflection.)

Read the Prelude aloud (pp. 1–2), perhaps noting the prophetic nature of this piece, given the economic, environmental, and leadership challenges our international communities face at this time. Then invite participants to take the next ten minutes *in silence* to reflect and write on this notion of the rope that helps us find our way home in the blizzards of our lives. Here are some possible open and honest questions for journaling and reflection:

What experiences have you had of actual blizzards? What are they like?

Speaking metaphorically, what blizzards have you known in your life?

What is "home" for you?

What or who is the rope that helps you find "home"?

Reading of the Touchstones: Establishing the Ground Rules for Discussion

Chapter V of *A Hidden Wholeness* stresses the need for clear limits in a circle of trust. (You may want to suggest reading pages 73–75.) Here is a version of the touchstones that the Courage community uses in our circles. We recommend that you give each person a copy and read them aloud at each session:

Circle of Trust Touchstones

- *Extend and receive welcome.* People learn best in hospitable spaces. In this circle, we support each other's learning by giving and receiving hospitality.

- *Be present as fully as possible.* Be here with your doubts, fears, and failings as well as your convictions, joys, and successes, your listening as well as your speaking.

- *What is offered in the circle is by invitation, not demand.* This is not a "share or die" event! During this retreat, do whatever your soul calls for, and know that you do it with our support. Your soul knows your needs better than we do.

- *Speak your truth in ways that respect other people's truth.* Our views of reality may differ, but speaking one's truth in a circle of trust does not mean interpreting, correcting, or debating what others say. Speak from your center to the center of the circle, using "I" statements, trusting people to do their own sifting and winnowing.

- *No fixing, no saving, no advising, and no setting each other straight.* This is one of the hardest guidelines for those of us in the "helping professions." But it is one of the most vital rules if we wish to make a space that welcomes the soul, the inner teacher.

- *Learn to respond to others with honest, open questions instead of counsel or corrections.* With such questions, we help "hear each other into deeper speech."

- *When the going gets rough, turn to wonder.* If you feel judgmental or defensive, ask yourself, "I wonder, what might have brought her to this belief?" or "What is he feeling right now?" or "What does my reaction teach me about myself?" Set aside judgment to listen to others—and to yourself—more deeply.

- *Attend to your own inner teacher.* We learn from others, of course. But as we explore poems, stories, questions, and silence in a circle of trust, we have a special opportunity to learn from within. So pay close attention to your own reactions and responses, to your most important teacher.

- *Trust and learn from the silence.* Silence is a gift in our noisy world and a way of knowing in itself. Treat silence as a member of the group. After someone has spoken, take time to reflect without immediately filling the space with words.

- *Observe deep confidentiality.* Trust comes from knowing that group members honor confidences and take seriously the ethics of privacy and discretion.

- *Know that it's possible to leave the circle with whatever it was that you needed when you arrived.* Know that the seeds planted here can keep growing in the days ahead.

Group Sharing

Although the members of your group may know each other, this first session offers an opportunity to model a countercultural mode of self-introduction, one that is not about what we do or where we work, our external selves or roles, but about our inner selves and souls. Here also is an opportunity to show that everything in this circle is invitational, that it is not "share or die" (see p. 78). Invite an insight from individuals' reflections about the rope or the blizzard. Each person speaks when ready: we never march in lockstep around the circle, pressuring people to say something; we let individuals enter when and if they wish to do so.

Closing Circle

The DVD included with this book offers the opportunity to listen to Parker Palmer speak about many ideas in *A Hidden Wholeness*. After each person is invited to speak into the circle what the session has meant personally, we suggest ending this session with Chapter 1 of the DVD, "The Primacy of Soul" (4:00 min.).

Chapter I: Images of Integrity: Living "Divided No More" (pp. 3–11)

Welcome and Reflection

Begin this session with the Douglas Wood quote on jack pines (p. 3). Then invite participants to reflect or journal on these questions for ten minutes in silence:

> Where in your life and work do you feel most whole? Where do you feel a sense of integrity that comes from a sense of "being what you are"?
>
> Where do you feel most divided, "so far removed from the truth we hold within that we cannot know the 'integrity that comes from being what you are'" (p. 4)?

Touchstones

We suggest using the touchstones in some form at each session, being clear that you are very intentional in setting the boundaries that create safe space for the soul to show up. You may want to vary the way you do this each time when you see the note "Read the touchstones." Sometimes you may choose to read them all or invite participants to read them aloud; sometimes you may want to highlight selected ones; at other times you might invite several group members to each share one that is especially important to them.

Group Sharing

Invite participants to form pairs, giving them ten minutes to talk about insights that came during their journaling and reminding them that this is not a "share or die" event; no one is compelled to share anything unless he or she chooses to do so. This is not to be the usual "ping-pong" conversation; each member of a pair has five minutes to speak without interruption, while the other listens attentively. When the ten minutes are up, regather the large group to hear from those who wish to share, reminding people to speak only for themselves rather than to quote their partners.

Closing Circle

After sharing comments into the closing circle, viewing Chapter 5 on the DVD, "Establishing Conditions for Circles of Trust" (5:37 min.), offers your group a chance to consider the conditions necessary for a circle of trust. This will allow participants to hear about the kind of environment they are already beginning to experience. You will be discussing these conditions in detail later in the book group (Chapter V), but we suggest using this section to offer the group a clearer sense of the process.

Additional Possibilities for This Chapter

We have included a few "additional possibilities" for every chapter in case you want to do something different than the design we have proposed, you want your sessions to be longer than our design assumes, or you decide to offer more sessions than the ten we outline in this guide. Here are two possibilities for Chapter I:

1. What does John Middleton Murry's remark, "It is better to be whole than to be good" (p. 8), mean to you? Tell a story about how this insight has come to life for you, either in yourself or in someone you know.

2. Reread the words on page 9: "Lovelier still [than the jack pine] is the sight of a man or woman standing with integrity intact. Speak the names of Rosa Parks or Nelson Mandela—or other names known nowhere but within your own grateful heart—and you catch a glimpse of the beauty that arises when people refuse to live divided lives." Who comes to mind when you read this statement? What are some of the qualities you think about when naming that person? What has knowing that person evoked within you? What do such qualities bring to the world?

Chapter II: Across the Great Divide: Rejoining Soul and Role (pp. 13–29)

Welcome and Reflection

Begin this session with Chapter 2 of the DVD, "The Great Divide" (4:28 min.). Then invite participants to turn to page 25 in *A Hidden Wholeness* and listen as you (or another group member) read aloud the words about the inner teacher and the paradox of the journey toward that inner truth being too difficult to undergo alone. (Begin with the last paragraph on page 25 and end with the three bulleted points on page 26.) Let the words take your group into a few minutes of silent reflection.

There are several passages in this chapter that can serve as wonderful third things for evoking memories of childhood and listening for one's own gifts, one's calling. You may want to read aloud a paragraph or two (pp. 14–15) about the early appearance of the instinct to protect ourselves by living divided, about how we deal with the painful gap between soul and role. Then invite participants to reflect and journal for about ten minutes in silence on how they used to play as children, using these questions to frame the reflection:

- Let yourself remember where you most often played. Was it in nature, your room, the backyard? Did you have favorite games, friends (real or imaginary), toys, stories? Did you have a secret life of play and imagination? What gifts or interests might be reflected in your childhood play?

- How do you play now? Have your childhood play and interests carried into adulthood in ways you may not have considered before? Whether or not they have, how does it feel to compare your life of play and imagination as an adult to the one you had as a child?

Touchstones

Read the touchstones.

Group Sharing

Invite participants to speak into the circle—reminding them that this is an invitation, not a requirement—naming aloud a memory or an insight from their writing. Suggest that group members listen for whatever hints of gifts and life directions might be embedded in these early memories and experiences. Invite the group to journal for a few minutes on the question of whether anything or anyone has separated or cut them off from their birthright gifts.

Closing Circle

After all who choose to do so have shared insights into the circle, end this session by inviting different voices to read the story about a man in a retreat struggling with racism, starting with the paragraph beginning "Here is another story . . ." on page 27 and finishing with the paragraph on page 28 that starts with "If we want to renew . . ." In addition to bringing closure to this session, this reading provides a segue into the next two sessions.

Additional Possibilities for This Chapter

1. The story of the man who realized that he "reports to the land" (pp. 18–19) offers another third thing to help participants remember their own stories. Read this story aloud, and then invite members to journal for ten to fifteen minutes on the following topic:

   > Think about a time when someone you know made a stand like the farmer, a time when he or she decided to live "divided no more," when it became clear that the person "reports to the land." It may have been one of your children, a coworker, or a partner. Or it might be your own story about a time when you reconnected your soul with your role. Tell that story in your journal.

   Then invite anyone who wishes to share his or her stories or insights with the group.

2. On page 18, we read about how we choose against wholeness by slipping into the familiar patterns of evasion: denial, equivocation, fear, cowardice, and avarice. After reading that selection aloud, invite reflection and journaling on the following question: Have you watched yourself, a friend, your partner, your child, a colleague, or one of your peers lead a divided life? Without naming the person, describe what you noticed, how the dividedness manifested itself in that person's (or your own) actions, words, behaviors, or feelings.

Chapter III: Explorations in True Self: Intimations of the Soul (pp. 31–49)

Welcome and Reflection

Read the passage about "spiritual DNA" (p. 32). Then invite participants to remember and journal about the gifts and qualities that have been with them since childhood—their own spiritual DNA. Some of these gifts may have surfaced in their writing during the last session, when they considered childhood play. Also note that we can gain some insight by remembering what others who know us well have said to us all of our lives, things such as "You are so intuitive" or "You listen so deeply to others" or "I rely on your creativity." Allow some time for journaling on these questions:

> How might you name and claim your birthright gifts, your own spiritual DNA?
>
> What gifts have others often mirrored back to you?

Touchstones

Read the touchstones.

Group Sharing

Invite people to share some of the insights about gifts named in their reflections. To continue your exploration of the terrain of "true self" or soul, read aloud the section on pages 33–34 that starts with the line "Philosophers haggle . . ." and ends with the fourth bullet, the section about the many names for "true self" and the functions of the soul. Here are some suggested questions for journaling and discussion:

- How do you nurture true self? What conditions support your soul's well-being? What does your soul yearn for and need in order to thrive and guide your life?

- What conditions conspire to silence your soul's voices and hungers? How do you conspire to silence your soul, conspire in your own diminishment? Can you think of a particular time when you did so?

Closing Circle

After sharing insights into the circle, use Chapter 3 of the DVD, "The Journey Toward an Undivided Life" (6:46 min.), to listen to the description of the Möbius strip, also described in this chapter.

Additional Possibilities for This Chapter

1. To explore the Möbius strip further (pp. 39–49), invite your participants to make a strip of their own, creating the four stages themselves, giving them enough time for reflection on each stage of "life on the Möbius strip." Consider the following questions:

   - In what ways do I consciously cocreate something life-giving as my inner and outer life merge into each other, and what are the conditions under which that is most likely to happen?

   - In what ways do I consciously cocreate something death-dealing as my inner and outer life merge into each other, and what are the conditions under which that is most likely to happen?

   - What are the places or situations in my life where I try to hide behind a wall rather than live in a consciously cocreative way on the Möbius strip?

2. Begin by reading aloud Mary Oliver's understanding about the soul (p. 34). Use a strip of paper to demonstrate the four phases of the Möbius strip (or show again the segment of the DVD where this is demonstrated). Now give each person a strip of paper and a piece of tape:

   - Read aloud the first three paragraphs on page 32, and ask participants to write three or four of their birthright gifts on one side of the strip of paper.

   - Then ask participants to write on the other side a few words or phrases that describe their work in the world.

   - Now invite them to form a Möbius strip with the paper and notice the seamless way each flows into and cocreates the other.

3. Journal about a time when you knew your inner and outer life were integrated on the Möbius strip. Journal about a time when your inner and outer worlds felt cut off from each other, when you felt you were living a divided life.

Chapter IV: Being Alone Together:
A Community of Solitudes (pp. 51–69)

Welcome and Reflection

This chapter, on the paradox of being alone in community, describes our need both for the life-giving qualities of solitude and for communities that support the voice of the soul. Ask participants to take ten to fifteen minutes to journal in response to the following questions:

> Have you ever been a part of a community, group, or relationship that "invaded or threatened your soul" or sent your soul into hiding? What can you say about the experience that violated your inner life?

> Have you been part of a community, group, or relationship that was hospitable to your soul? What was it about that experience that worked for you, that allowed your soul to show up?

Touchstones

Read the touchstones.

Group Sharing

Before you invite participants to break into triads to share reflections from their journaling, set forth a few guidelines for that time. (1) Each person talks for about five minutes, during which the two others listen respectfully, with no comments or questions, no agreeing or disagreeing, no "ping-pong" conversation. (2) After all three participants in each triad have spoken, they should reflect together on whether there were common elements in the stories that were inviting to the soul or in those that scared the soul away. Then return to the large circle to share insights or observations.

Closing Circle

Invite people to read aloud a phrase or sentence from this chapter that resonated with them and share, if they wish, why those words touched them. Finally, invite general insights or comments about what people might be taking away from this session.

Additional Possibilities for This Chapter

If you want to go deeper with your group, you might use these poems as third things:

1. "Making Contact" by Virginia Satir, in *Teaching with Fire* (p. 123). Read the poem aloud. Then use these questions for journaling, or pose your own questions:
   - What speaks to you in the poem?
   - What do you know about feeling seen or heard by another person or seeing or hearing another person?

Recommended Resources

Teaching with Fire: Poetry That Sustains the Courage to Teach, ed. Sam M. Intrator and Megan Scribner (2003). A superb collection of eighty-eight poems from such beloved writers as Walt Whitman, Langston Hughes, Mary Oliver, Billy Collins, Emily Dickinson, and Pablo Neruda. Each of these evocative poems is accompanied by a brief story from a teacher explaining the significance of the poem in his or her life's work.

Leading from Within: Poetry That Sustains the Courage to Lead, ed. Sam M. Intrator and Megan Scribner (2007). Another superb collection of ninety-three poems chosen by leaders from various walks of life and accompanied by brief personal commentaries explaining the personal and professional meaning of the poem.

---

2. "The Way It Is" by William Stafford, in *Leading from Within* (p. 11). After reading the poem aloud, offer questions such as these for reflection:

- How would you name the thread you follow, the thread that marks your path on the Möbius strip?

- What or who helps you follow that thread and never let go?

Chapter V: Preparing for the Journey: Creating Circles of Trust (pp. 71–87)

Welcome and Reflection

Chapter V explores the five essential features of a circle of trust: clear boundaries, skilled leadership, open invitation, common ground, and graceful ambiance. Begin this session by watching Chapter 4 of the DVD, "Circles of Trust" (4:32 min.), which discusses the different elements involved in creating such circles.

Invite reflections about *your* book group, asking participants to consider what circle of trust principles and practices have been most important for them in the meetings thus far. Take about ten minutes for journaling on these questions:

What, for you, are the essential elements in a circle of trust?

What practices have been important to the success of this circle of trust for you, practices that have felt hospitable to your soul?

Touchstones

Read the touchstones.

Group Sharing

Invite your group members to reflect aloud on their experience of these practices thus far. What do they think is indispensable for creating a circle of trust? Where would they as individuals like to grow in their use of these principles and practices?

Closing Circle

Chapter V also explores using the metaphors of the seasons to create common ground for long-term circles of trust. To close this session, ask each person to consider the question "What season am I in now?" Invite sharing, from those who wish, in the closing circle.

Additional Possibilities for This Chapter

1. More information on long-term, seasonally based circles of trust for various professional groups can be found on the Center for Courage & Renewal Web page (http://www.couragerenewal.org). You may also want to use the section on seasonal retreats on the DVD that accompanies the guide to the tenth anniversary edition of *The Courage to Teach*.

2. Read aloud the appropriate seasonal essay for the time of year in Chapter VI of *Let Your Life Speak*. Then invite participants to journal on the following questions:
   - What questions or images does this season offer me?
   - What speaks to me in this essay?
   - What can I learn from this season?

Chapter VI: The Truth Told Slant: The Power of Metaphor (pp. 89–111)

Welcome and Reflection

Chapter VI introduces the use of metaphors to give people access to inner-life issues. This method, which is at the heart of circles of trust, depends on the careful selection of third things such as poetry, stories, art, or music. Open this session with Chapter 7 on the

DVD (4:55 min.), "Common Ground & Third Things," to hear this practice discussed.

Touchstones

Read the touchstones.

Group Sharing

Although Chapter VI gives many examples and ideas for a process used in working with "The Woodcarver," reading the chapter can't provide the experience of actually working through this poem in a group. So offer your group the experience of what the Woodcarver calls "a live encounter" in the manner described in this chapter. Before the session begins, reread the chapter, with its detailed guidance on how to work with "The Woodcarver."

Read this story aloud (pp. 95–96) in a way that sets a reflective mood and pace for your time together. Then follow the suggestions on pages 97–111, beginning the discussion with the following questions:

What is this story about for you?

How does it intersect your life at this moment?

Then discuss each stanza, using the questions Palmer suggests to guide your group's journaling or conversation, or create your own questions for exploration.

Closing Circle

Invite participants to share one insight they had during their writing about "The Woodcarver." Ask:

What spoke to you in the poem?

What was meaningful to you in this session?

Additional Possibilities for This Chapter

1. Together, watch Chapter 9 of the DVD, "Inner Work Can Change the Outer World" (4:10 min.).

2. Invite journaling with questions such as these, followed by sharing in pairs or triads:

   - What is my bell stand?
   - Who is "the Highness" in my life?
   - What are the trees?
   - What questions does this poem leave with me?

3. Work with another poem in this manner, a poem that speaks to you. Consider these two possibilities from *Teaching with Fire:* "The Journey," by Mary Oliver (p. 59), or "Sweet Darkness," by David Whyte (p. 83).

Chapter VII: Deep Speaks to Deep: Learning to Speak and Listen (pp. 113–128)

Welcome and Reflection

Chapter VII explores ways of speaking and listening in a circle of trust, using rules that are often very different from everyday conversations, and distinguishes between instrumental speech and expressive speech. Open with Chapter 6 on the DVD, "Characteristics of a Circle of Trust" (4:55 min.).

Then invite participants to journal for ten to fifteen minutes, suggesting that they write a story of a time when someone tried to give advice or "fix" them—or when they tried to do the same for someone else. What happened as a result?

Touchstones

Read the touchstones.

Group Sharing

This chapter also notes the power of exploring the truth via our own stories, so invite people to share personal stories from their journal reflections.

Closing Circle

After sharing insights, feelings, or appreciations from the time spent together, read aloud the poem "Love After Love" (p. 86), and invite the group to consider aloud what it means to "feast on your life."

Additional Possibilities for This Chapter

1. Although you have used the poem "Love After Love" as a closing piece for your session, we invite you now to consider using the poem as a third thing. It is a rich poem to work with in ways similar to your use of "The Woodcarver" in an earlier session. You may want to reread Chapter VI, paying close attention to the part about using third things and to the suggestions for working with the poem. Ask your group members, as Palmer suggests in that chapter, "What is this poem about for you? How does it intersect your life at this moment? Is there a word, a phrase, or an image here that speaks directly to your condition?"

2. To go deeper into the art of listening, we suggest working with any of these poems in *Leading from Within:* William Stafford's "Listening" (p. 48), Hafiz's "How Do I Listen?" (p.176), or John Fox's "When Someone Deeply Listens to You" (p. 220). You will find suggestions for asking questions on page 222 of that book.

Chapter VIII: Living the Questions: Experiments with Truth (pp. 129–149)

Welcome and Reflection

Chapter VIII provides a description of the clearness committee discernment process, a central practice in creating circles of trust. Show the group Chapter 8 on the DVD, "The Clearness Committee" (6:22 min.), which provides a clear overview of this practice. Invite a few minutes of silence to reflect on the ideas and spirit of this Quaker practice.

Read the Touchstones

Read the touchstones.

Group Sharing

Clearness committees require us to abandon the pretense that we know what is best for another person. Instead, we ask honest, open questions that can help someone find his or her own answers. Questions of that sort require practice, so before your group decides to hold an actual clearness committee, create an opportunity to help participants develop this skill.

First, go through the guidelines for asking open and honest questions by reading pages 130–134 aloud. Then ask one person to volunteer a clearness committee issue to put before the group. Since most people will be new to this process and are likely to make mistakes, the issue should be one that is real for your focus person and yet not too personal, such as "What is the best design for a new course I have in mind?" or "What might be my next writing project?" Clearness committees are normally used to explore the deeper dilemmas of our lives—issues in the family or workplace, challenging relationships, or a fundamental concern about how we are living our lives. But in this situation, your goal is to provide the group a chance to practice without making the volunteer overly vulnerable.

The person states his or her dilemma, after which others write trial questions in their journals. Then the questions are asked one at a time, and the group is given a chance to comment on whether it is an open and honest question and if not, why it isn't and how it might be improved. The volunteer does not need to answer the questions; the purpose here is to learn to frame open and honest questions, not deal with a dilemma. But because the volunteer may be especially sensitive to questions that may seem "leading" or pushy, he or she should always feel invited to speak.

Ask that someone in the group write the questions down for the focus person so that he or she may use them for journaling and reflection. As you end this session, ask the participants to reflect on what they have noticed about the nature of trying to ask questions of this sort—where they felt challenged in forming them and what they learned about doing so. Learning to ask open and honest questions is demanding, but developing that skill can help strengthen and deepen many relationships.

Closing Circle

End your time by reading aloud the story of Virginia Shorey, beginning with the line "But it is never too late" (p. 147). Then invite participants to share their insights or reflections about this session in the circle.

Additional Possibilities for This Chapter

Now that the members of your group understand the care and skill required, they can decide whether they feel ready, willing, and able to conduct full-fledged clearness committees. The number of volunteers needed to serve as focus persons—if the whole book group wants to be involved—depends on the size of your group: each committee needs a minimum of four members and a maximum of six.

As leader, part of your job is to assign members to the committees, asking focus persons privately for the names of any persons whom they would prefer not to have on their committee—making it clear that you do not need to know their reasons. You will also need to make sure that suitable private spaces are available for your committees to meet simultaneously. Before the clearness committees meet, ask participants to review Chapter VIII with care to make sure they understand and can commit to the core principles and practices. A sample schedule for a committee is found on page 136 of *A Hidden Wholeness;* using that template, prepare a schedule to distribute to your group to give participants step-by-step guidance through the session.

The session itself will require a total of three hours: one hour for the leader to prepare the group for its work and deal with questions and concerns and two hours for the actual clearness committee meetings. Begin the first hour by viewing the section of the DVD titled "Extras: The Clearness Committee in Greater Detail" (25:30 min.), where you will find step-by-step instructions for the process. After viewing that section with the group, discuss any questions and concerns people may have, reminding them just before the committees begin of the critical "double confidentiality" rule.

When the committees end, this session is over. It would be good to spend some time at your next gathering debriefing the process—but never the content—in order to deepen all participants' understanding of what they learned from the process.

Chapter IX: On Laughter and Silence: Not-So-Strange Bedfellows (pp. 151–165)

Welcome and Reflection

Silence and laughter are essential ingredients of a circle of trust, as they are of any meaningful human relationship. Use this session to reflect with participants on the role of silence and laughter in their own lives and in their experience of this group.

Because silence is one of the topics for this session, begin by inviting the group to share five minutes of silence. At the end of that time, invite participants to journal on one or more of the following questions:

How would you describe your own relationship with silence or laughter (or both)?

Tell a story of a time when silence or laughter was a positive element in your community or personal life. Tell another story of a time when its impact was negative.

How have you experienced the role of silence or laughter in this group?

Touchstones

Read the touchstones.

Group Sharing

Break into groups of three for forty-five minutes. Each person has fifteen minutes to share anything he or she wishes from the journaling and then receive honest, open questions from the two listeners.

Closing Circle

Read the poem "I Believe in All That Has Never Been Spoken" by Rainer Maria Rilke, in *Teaching with Fire* (p. 177), or a poem of your choice that relates to these themes. Close the session by briefly sharing what the session has meant to each of you.

Additional Possibilities for This Chapter

1. We all have a different relationship with silence and perhaps a different capacity for it as well. But the devaluing of silence in our culture means that most of us need to develop our ability to be still. Invite participants to explore what silence means to them by having a "dialogue with silence" in their journals, perhaps something like this:

   Self: Silence, where have you been? I've missed having you in my life.

   Silence: I am always available, waiting for an invitation, waiting to be invited into your life. But I haven't heard from you in a long time? Why is that?

   Self: I meant to, but I kept putting it off. Why do I fear quieting down?

Continue journaling for twenty minutes, letting the dialogue unfold. Then invite people to return to the circle and share from their writing.

2. If you would like to continue exploring silence, you might use Pablo Neruda's "Keeping Quiet" in *Teaching with Fire* (p. 103). In the essay that accompanies the poem, Catherine Gerber comments on how Neruda's quiet is "not the silence of isolation but the quiet that connects us in community." Invite people to journal on the differences between the kinds of silence, recalling experiences of both kinds.

Chapter X: The Third Way:
Nonviolence in Everyday Life (pp. 167–186)

As you prepare to work with this last chapter of *A Hidden Wholeness*, think about the possibilities that lie ahead. The circle of trust experience your group has had may point toward new possibilities. Some participants may want to continue meeting on a regular basis, using other related writings. Some may want to share this way of gathering with others, starting new book groups with interested people. Some may want to sign up for a Circle of Trust® retreat through the Center for Courage & Renewal, a retreat offered not to prepare facilitators but to deepen people's experience with the principles and practices of the process.

Welcome and Reflection

Begin by reading aloud the section on a "third way" to respond to violence (top of p. 170). Give participants a few minutes to remember a story of a time when they responded in this way to a difficult situation and then five or ten more minutes to write about it in their journals.

Touchstones

Read the touchstones.

Group Sharing

Invite participants to move into triads for thirty minutes to share their reflections and stories about the "third way." Each person in the triad has ten minutes to share whatever he or she would like from the reflection and journaling, with no "ping-pong" conversation allowed. If an individual does not take the full ten minutes, ask the two listeners to use the remaining time to ask open, honest questions.

Closing Circle

Invite sharing in the large circle after the triads. First ask group members to reflect aloud on how they might take what they know about circles of trust into their personal and professional worlds. Then close with reflections on and celebrations of what this time together in a circle of trust has meant to the participants, ending the session with Chapter 11 on the DVD, "Nonviolence in Everyday Life" (4:26 min.).

Additional Possibilities for This Chapter

1. The idea of the tragic gap is one that offers rich possibilities for further exploration. You may want to take time for more reflection by reading the passages about the tragic gap and the often painful result of having our hearts broken open (pp. 174–181).

   Then watch Chapter 10 of the DVD, "Standing in the Tragic Gap" (4:52 min.). Encourage participants to take some time to think about the tragic gaps in their lives—and to write about them in their journals for fifteen minutes. Use questions such as these to frame the journaling:

   - Where do you stand in a tragic gap in your life, your home, your work, your community?

   - How do you name the tensions of those gaps?

   - What makes it difficult to stand in the gap, faithfully holding that tension? What helps you do so?

- How do you guard your spirit when standing in the tragic gap?

- Do you know anyone who models, better than most, how to stand in the tragic gap? What are the qualities that allow that person to do so?

After the journaling, invite people to share these reflections with each other in the large circle.

2. Read aloud the story of John Woolman on pages 180–181, and invite a group discussion about how this story brings to life the notion of the tragic gap. Here are some possible discussion questions:

- In the story we read that Woolman, a tailor, "received a revelation from God that slavery was an abomination and that Friends should set their slaves free." Have you ever received a revelation that set you against the current of your community? What was the nature of that revelation, and how did you proceed with it? What have you learned about what sustains you, what is life-giving, while holding the tensions and complexity in the tragic gap?

- In your life, in your heart and soul, what are the issues that might call forth this sort of dedication and discipline in you today?

PART III:
TAKING INNER WORK
INTO OUR OUTER WORLDS

"If it ain't in your heart, it ain't in your horn."
—CHARLIE PARKER

Now that you have experienced a circle of trust book group shaped by the ideas in *A Hidden Wholeness*, you or people in your group may be actively exploring the question "How do we take these principles and practices into our lives outside the circle?" It is a question with many answers. In fact, once we have experienced this way of being with other people, it is hard to return to "business as usual" in any relationship.

Taking this way of being into the outer world does not require creating a program or leading a retreat. We need only go about what we are already doing in new ways. In business meetings, for instance, we can ask open, honest questions in an effort to understand another's viewpoint instead of simply objecting to what he or she has said. With our children or our students, we can listen more deeply and ask questions instead of giving answers—and respond to *their* answers with curiosity rather than judgment.

Behaviors of this sort can bring new life to groups and institutions as well as individuals because they help build trust—and collective work of any sort is done better when the people doing the work trust each other. In every situation, we can ask ourselves, Are my words and actions enhancing or undermining relational trust? Am I honoring the souls of the people I am with?—questions that can be asked only by people who have learned to honor their own souls.

As we have facilitated Circles of Trust® over the past decade, we have often asked participants, "How have you changed as a result of your experience? What do you now do differently?"

Here are some of the responses we have received (including our own) in the participants' own words. As we bring this guide to a close, we offer these stories in hopes of sparking your imagination—and the imaginations of the people in your circle—about how the experience of a circle of trust can be taken into the larger world as we continue to live "life on the Möbius strip."

Joy in an Imperfect World

Sally Z. Hare, a teacher and Courage facilitator, feels able to live life with more attention and intention, more clarity and awareness.

> I am more intentional about what I say, what I do, and how I "be." Whether I am fixing dinner or walking the dogs or writing an article, I am more present. I see and feel the difference in how I ask questions, listen, create the space for myself, and guard my own spirit in everyday things. I give careful attention to my relationships so they have the best chance of being positive, loving, and mutually beneficial places of growth.
>
> Another significant change for me is more clarity about what I say yes to and, equally important, what I say no to. Part of living this way is recognizing the abundance in my life and taking the time to reflect on and express my gratitude. I have more clarity about what is life-giving for me and what is not. I have come to accept, even to embrace, that living in the tragic gap comes with being human in this world. I will always see differences between reality and the way things can be, but I don't have to feel despair. My work is standing in that gap and holding both poles of the paradoxes of life. I no longer get overwhelmed by it in the same way. It's not that the gaps are no longer there; they're always there. But I have increased my capacity for joy in chaos and embracing paradox. I love my life. I love what I do. I love being who I am in this time and place. I love being in this imperfect world.

The Metaphor of the Singing Meditation Bowl

Ruth Shagoury, a teacher education professor and writer, has found ways to deepen community in her classes, inviting stories, sharing poetry, and creating space for silence. Although she acknowledges the difficult working conditions that still exist for her in higher education, she now brings herself to her classroom, never losing her playfulness and creativity.

I have always loved poetry and stories, but I now feel I have permission to make them central in my teaching. What is essential is connecting what I am teaching to the students' lives, to *their* inner teachers. In academe, students come in thinking they are supposed to write in a distanced and disembodied academic voice; I invite them to tell a story in their own words and grounded in their own experience. Community then becomes possible, and the learning goes deeper.

As a result of Courage work, I teach my students that silence is OK in my classroom. I bring my meditation bowl to the class and ring it before beginning, allowing time for the bowl to resonate and become still. This singing meditation bowl is a metaphor for Courage work: it calls out to us yet welcomes the silence and is the transition for going deeper in community. That sound of the bowl that lingers so long; you learn to sit quietly, waiting for it to come to you. It is a paradox, calming and yet exciting at the same time.

When I teach reading comprehension, instead of lecturing on the power of books in our lives, I begin by inviting students to tell a story of a book that changed their lives. One woman told of a time when she was unable to afford college and was working as a waitress, but she was also reading *Walden II;* as a result, she joined a commune and lived there for five years! We never would have known this about her had she not told this story, and her story demonstrated how reading changes lives.

I use poems like "Shoulders" by Naomi Shihab Nye (in *Teaching with Fire,* p. 163), a poem about a man carrying a young child safely across a busy, rainy street. I ask open and honest, evocative questions of my students, like "Who is on your shoulders at this time?" and "Who are you carrying in your work and lives?"

Then I also invite them to tell a story of a time when someone carried them, when they were on someone else's shoulders. Then we share the writing. I remember one student noting afterward that she couldn't have imagined telling this story as she did and being listened to as she was.

Another student in this class was a bit brittle and difficult to work with. In this "Shoulders" session, she told the story of her husband leaving her with six children while she was supporting them on a middle school teacher's salary. She noted that colleagues carried her on their shoulders and brought her food when she felt she was falling apart. Many people at the school didn't know what was going on for her, but these colleagues did. She reflected that her students have their stories too, stories we often don't know about. Stories create compassion and sensitivity toward each other and toward the students we serve. Storytelling takes things from the general to the particular, where the real learning happens. And especially exciting to me, I see my students come to embody these principles and pass them on to their students in their classrooms.

I wish I could say I had more tips for academia—it is a hard place to work. I have come to accept that we can't completely change the culture of these places, but we can have better tools to work within them and with our own reactions. I have less self-doubt in academe, even though I do not have a traditional scholarly voice. This work has allowed my true self to show up more, my passion, creativity, and playfulness. I no longer hide from the class. This is who I am.

Life at the Center of the Duck Pond

Faye Orton Snyder, a pastor and seminary educator, feels that circles of trust have transformed her ministry from the inside out. She describes a new sense of energy and peace and a new level of trust and acceptance in her congregation. She has also changed how she works with seminary students.

This Courage work is the real deal. I feel more awake than I ever have. I have gas in the tank all of the time, I tell my friends. I also have a sense of calm in my life, because I am honoring my desire for silence, spending more time in nature, and journaling daily. My own soul work is in place.

After the first retreat I attended, I realized the importance of vulnerability and honesty in my leadership. A congregation can be like a teenager, probing and prodding until they know you are authentic and connected to something larger. But once they find that in you, they accept you. It reminds me of ice-skating on a frozen duck pond when I was a little girl. My friends and I would stand at the edges, and if the ice seemed unstable, we wouldn't skate out to the middle. But the ice is always more solid in the middle than on the edges of the pond. Many clergy are like that with their roles and their congregations: they test the edges, which seem unstable, and soon are afraid to risk the vulnerability of skating to the middle, of leading from within, from their own truth and integrity. But staying on the edges, hiding behind roles, and not involving our deepest selves out of a misguided desire to protect ourselves is where burnout happens. Ministry is about trusting your congregation and yourself and getting out to the center.

The inward attention to poetry in circles of trust has opened me up to richer language for public prayer. I have come to appreciate silence and have added it to our worship service, giving the members of the congregation time to catch up with themselves.

In my preaching, I have come to see myself as my own best resource rather than always turning to outside sources. In the early 1980s, I was taught deductive preaching in seminary, where you tell a story and make three points, or use what I call the "gobble and spit approach," where you read as much as you can and regurgitate it on Sunday morning. Now I use the lectionary as a third thing. I ask open and honest questions of the text, and everything I need to say comes from that and from my own inner teacher. I see sermons as instruments of transformation. I don't think people want to know more— they want to experience something of the holy.

When I coach seminarians, I ask them to sit with a sermon topic and text for two or three hours, asking open and honest questions of the text and finding related stories in their own lives, so they can stand and preach in confidence from their own truth. Sometimes I ask them to stand in front of their notes and talk directly to us. My students are grateful when they realize they can do this. In supervising the student interns, I use open and honest questions, which engender more questions, and supervision becomes much more fun!

What seminarians starting out in ministry lack more than anything is an inner self-confidence. This approach supports them in finding their own voices. When the semester ends, I give each student a copy of *Let Your Life Speak!*

Pizza Parties and the Power of Mirrors

David Hagstrom, an educational leader, consultant, author, and storyteller, uses the practices learned in circles of trust to deepen his own skills of listening, mirroring, and asking questions. He creates soul-safe spaces for isolated school leaders to come together as resources for each other.

Being immersed in this work has fine-tuned my listening, especially through asking open and honest questions and offering mirroring and affirmations in my everyday relationships. No matter who I meet, I cannot help myself—I ask questions. I have always been a community builder (I have been doing it for over fifty years!), but I would have been much more effective had I known about this work sooner. I started realizing that when I am in a conversation about a difficulty, a stuck place, a problem, I feel pressure to offer my best advice, the best I can give to the other person. Then I realized that a better gift is simply mirroring back what I heard and saw. I started doing it, and was surprised at the outset to hear afterward, "No one has ever done that for me, has provided this mirror." Later, people would come back and say, "You know, that mirroring of what you saw and heard was probably the most helpful stuff in terms of moving myself along with my problem." For me, in my fifty years in school leadership, nothing else worked very well. We admire the exemplary models of how to be strong, sturdy, great leaders—but in terms of moving us along our own paths, the only way I have discovered that really helps is this practice. Since getting involved in the Courage community, I no longer engage others by sharing good ideas or making suggestions. I just try to fine-tune the questions, which is an art in itself, and to engage by trying to make my mirroring better, tighter, more careful.

As part of my love for the central Oregon schools, I started getting school principals together once a month from 5:00 to 8:00 P.M. for pizza and wine. Initially, it was simply a social occasion, but it became clear to me that while it was dandy to just chat, we could do some "circle work" here. School leaders are very isolated and face huge problems daily, often all on their own. We started with simple things like how to ask open and honest questions to support one another in discernment and then started doing walk-and-talks, and eventually I taught the whole clearness committee process. We soon realized that we needed more time, so we got together for a Saturday and eventually started offering retreats. These were opportunities for these folks to break the isolation they were feeling and be there for one another in ways that were extremely helpful.

Vocational Discernment in Community

Paul Kottke, a United Methodist minister, has used clearness committees in making decisions about vocational changes and about whether to become more involved in the national church. He attributes his sense of peace to his work in circles of trust and describes the way he has been seen anew by members of his congregation.

To use Christian language, I felt born again from my experience with circles of trust and clearness committees. The clearness committee is a powerful spiritual direction tool that has helped me in my own discernment process with my vocation. I had been asked to go to another church in the area, a big church. I didn't want to do it, but I wanted to honor the process and people, so it wasn't a clear no for me either. As a result of the clearness committee, I was able to make clear to the members of the interview team exactly what I would do if I came to their church. I was able to deal with them in a nondefensive way, and they and I both realized that I was not the candidate they wanted.

I was also wrestling with a fair amount of pressure to get engaged in the national church organization, something I was hesitant to do. Early on, I said no because of my children, and deep down, I never felt it was what God wanted me to do. Still, I hesitated. In the retreat series, I was able to wrestle with this over time, eventually coming to a definitive discernment. Through the clearness process, it became evident to me that I am not called in the national direction; my passion is for soul work grounded in an interfaith community as a way of engaging the public. That's what's happening in my city, anchored in my church and in the university. This discernment allowed me to say a clear no to national denominational work and yes to the emerging new thing. This new interfaith direction is not well defined and a little scary, but I have a feeling that I will look back and see my decision as a defining moment for me. Right now, I am not sure what will happen. The other choices were clearer and perhaps safer, but they did not connect to my passion.

As a result of these circles of trust, I feel reconnected with my soul, and a state of peace has emerged. There are several layers of alignment with soul: soul to soul, soul to role, soul to public engagement. It is this work that helped me articulate this alignment. Parishioners tell me, "I see a difference in you, a sense of clarity."

Welcoming Paradox and Complexity

Jay Casbon, a professor and retired university president, values going deeper through open questions and deep listening. He has developed an appreciation for the complexity of paradox and welcomes the tension and discomfort as a place for growth.

> As a result of this work, I look for ways to deepen conversations, projects, everything I do. I ask myself, What is the deeper take on this? I value the questions I carry from the many experiences I have had with clearness committees. I realize that open and honest questions work as well in everyday situations as they do in a clearness committee. In fact, the people I am with don't even need to know what I am doing. If I ask good questions and focus on really listening, I can deepen what is happening in everything that I do.
>
> This work has also given me a keen appreciation for paradox. Even though paradox often comes with great tension, discomfort, and loss of clarity, I have learned, when I catch sight of it, to welcome it as a liminal space, a place where we can break through illusion and eventually gain more clarity. I believe that once we create spaces for paradoxical conversations, for being consciously uncomfortable together, we can hold and even welcome complexity, which is often where there is the most growth.

The Robin and the Tiger Beetle

Caryl Hurtig Casbon, an interfaith minister and Courage facilitator, creates sacred spaces for the soul through circles of trust.

> Circles of trust have grounded me in "soul literacy"—an understanding of how the soul communicates, of how to invite, access, and listen to her wild voice. She speaks through intuition, or a silent knowing, evoked through literature, solitude, and the right questions—if I live like the robins. You know how robins run about eight inches, then stop, cock their heads, and look and listen? If nourishment is there, they find it. My soul offers continual guidance and sustenance, if only I will stop and listen, often. But we live in a culture that is more like the tiger beetle, which is the fastest land animal known in relation to its size—with one prob-

lem: when running toward its destination, it goes blind! How often have I approached my life like a tiger beetle! But after twelve years spent in circles of trust, the robin and tiger beetle are in better balance within me.

I've always had a great hunger for an inner life. But before I found the Courage community, I thought this need might be self-indulgent. Now I understand my hunger as healthy, vital to keeping my soul nourished as it informs my outer actions in the world. Contemplative time supports becoming self-aware, slowing down, and making choices that are life-giving. Courage work has taught me some of the how-to's of loving: deep listening, witnessing and honoring others, practices of nonviolence, and ways of handling complexity. It has been life-saving and life-shaping in so many ways.

I will never forget the first time I sat in a circle of trust facilitated by Parker Palmer—I felt I had come home. What this process gives me is permission to do what I came into this life to do: create meaningful, sacred spaces in community where people can touch and speak from a place of deep knowing within themselves. To witness this happening is a holy thing, for there is a great hunger and need for this kind of knowing, discernment, and connection in our world. Circles of trust offer practices that are respectful and trustworthy and a community of people who speak the language of the soul. This is the community to which I belong, the place that I can call home.

About the DVD

How to Use This DVD

The "Circles of Trust" DVD offers a thoughtful approach to professionals in many fields, and to anyone seeking ways to sustain personal integrity and courage amid the challenges of our time. It will inspire the viewer and strengthen his or her capacity to understand and introduce Circles of Trust principles and practices in schools, congregations, hospitals, workplaces, and communities.

With its menu-rich depth and versatility, this DVD can easily be adapted to busy lives and used in a wide variety of ways—at home or in the workplace, alone or in community:

- **As a way of sharing** or introducing the ideas and approaches to "rejoining soul and role" articulated by Parker J. Palmer in *A Hidden Wholeness* and practiced by Parker and the Center for Courage & Renewal at Circle of Trust retreats.
- **As a "third thing,"** a conversational centerpiece with which to foster rich dialogue and deeper understanding about the journey toward "living divided no more."
- **As a resource** for incorporating the principles and practices behind Circles of Trust into your personal and family life, workplace, and community.
- **As an adaptable tool** to be used in any way that supports and strengthens your ability to live more authentically, to "reconnect who you are with what you do."

How the Material Is Organized

The Circles of Trust DVD is organized into three movements, each of which is divided into short chapters that can be viewed independently, sequentially, or creatively combined.

The Soul—Explorations in True Self

In our frantic, fragmented, and often violent world, we can easily become separated from our own souls. What is it that drives "true self" into hiding? When we have lost track of ourselves, how can we find our way home?

1. The Primacy of Soul [4:00]
2. The Great Divide [4:28]
3. The Journey Toward an Undivided Life [6:46]

In Practice—Creating a Community of Solitudes

What does the journey toward wholeness require? Where can we find fellow travelers to support us along the way?

4. Circles of Trust [4:32]
5. Establishing Conditions for Circles of Trust [5:37]
6. Characteristics of a Circle of Trust [4:55]
7. Common Ground & Third Things [4:55]
8. The Clearness Committee [6:22]

In the World—Reconnecting Soul and Role

How does reconnecting with the soul make a difference in the world? Why is this work important to anyone besides the person who does it?

9. Inner Work Can Change the Outer World [4:10]
10. Standing in the Tragic Gap [4:52]
11. Nonviolence in Everyday Life [4:26]
12. The Soul of the Citizen [4:16]

Extras

A Conversation with Parker J. Palmer, Rick Jackson, and Marcy Jackson, co-directors of the Center for Courage & Renewal [29:38]

The Clearness Committee in Greater Detail [25:30]

Credits [1:39]

www.couragerenewal.org
@ 2008 The Center for Courage & Renewal
Digital Media & Design: Rollingbay Works, Dan Kowalski & Associates
Original Music by Christian Arthur

THE PROMISE OF PARADOX

A Celebration of Contradictions
in the Christian Life

Parker J. Palmer

Introduction by Henri Nouwen

ISBN 978-0-7879-9696-3
Hardcover

"The issues that Parker discusses are basic: solitude, community, social action, political responsibility, prayer, and contemplation...I hope and pray that those who read these essays will sense the spirit in which they were written and thus be challenged as I have been to break out of illusions and compulsions and seek a new freedom."

—From the Introduction by **Henri J.M. Nouwen**

First published in 1980—and reissued here with a feisty new introductory essay—*The Promise of Paradox* launched Parker J. Palmer's career as an author and his ongoing exploration of the contradictions that vex and enrich our lives. In this probing and heartfelt book, the distinguished writer, teacher, and activist examines some of the challenging questions at the core of Christian spirituality.

Animated by the insights of the Trappist monk Thomas Merton, *The Promise of Paradox* explores spiritual questions in the open and generous spirit of Christian mysticism, challenging forms of Christianity that are closed and even cruel. There are no easy answers to these questions, and there may be no answers at all. But with the poet Rainer Maria Rilke, Palmer advocates the rich possibilities that emerge when we learn to "live the questions."

THE COURAGE TO TEACH

Exploring the Inner Landscape of a
Teacher's Life

10ᵗʰ Anniversary Edition

Parker J. Palmer

ISBN 978-0-7879-9686-4
Hardcover/CD

"This book is for teachers who have good days and bad—and whose bad days bring the suffering that comes only from something one loves. It is for teachers who refuse to harden their hearts, because they love learners, learning, and the teaching life."

—From the Introduction by **Parker J. Palmer**

In the tenth anniversary edition of his classic *The Courage to Teach*, Parker J. Palmer offers hope, encouragement, and guidance to teachers—and other professionals—who want to recover the heart of their vocation and calling. His new Foreword reflects on ten years of "courage work," which has spread beyond education to help teachers and other professionals recover meaning and depth in their work lives. And a new concluding chapter takes a fresh look at a new kind of professional and what it means to "take heart" in one's work.

BONUS: Includes an audio CD featuring a forty-five minute conversation between Parker Palmer and his colleagues Marcy Jackson and Estrus Tucker from the Center for Courage & Renewal (www.CourageRenewal.org). They reflect on what they have learned from working with thousands of teachers in their "Courage to Teach" program and with others who yearn for greater integrity in their professional lives.

ALSO BY PARKER J. PALMER

THE COURAGE TO TEACH GUIDE FOR REFLECTION AND RENEWAL

10th Anniversary Edition

Parker J. Palmer

ISBN 978-0-7879-9687-1
Paperback/DVD

An important text and audio-visual resource from the best-selling author of *The Courage to Teach* for readers who want to "explore the inner landscape of a teacher's life" in ways that will make a difference for them, their students, their colleagues, and their institutions.

This extensively updated and expanded guide will help readers, individually and in groups, reflect on their teaching and renew their sense of vocation. The *Guide* proposes practical ways to create "safe space" for honest reflection and conversation, and offers chapter-by-chapter questions and exercises to explore the many insights in *The Courage to Teach*.

BONUS DVD: Brings *The Courage to Teach* alive through a seventy-minute interview with Parker J. Palmer, originally recorded as a resource for the Center for Courage & Renewal (www.CourageRenewal.org). Here he reflects on a wide range of subjects—including the heart of the teacher, the crisis in education, diverse ways of knowing, relationships in teaching and learning, spirituality in education, approaches to institutional transformation, and teachers as culture heroes. Discussion questions related to the topics explored on the DVD have been integrated into the *Guide*, giving individuals and study groups a chance to have "a conversation with the author" as well as an engagement with the text.

LET YOUR LIFE SPEAK

Listening for the Voice of Vocation

Parker J. Palmer

ISBN 978-0-7879-4735-4
Hardcover

"Clear, vital, honest. . . . Immerse yourself in the wisdom of these pages and allow it to carry you toward a more attentive relationship with your deeper, truer self."
—**John S. Mogabgab**, editor, *Weavings* Journal

Discover Your Path in Life

Let Your Life Speak is an insightful and moving meditation on finding one's true calling. The book's title is a time-honored Quaker admonition, usually taken to mean "Let the highest truths and values guide everything you do." But Palmer reinterprets those words, drawing on his own search for selfhood. "Before you tell your life what you intend to do with it," he writes, "listen for what it intends to do with you. Before you tell your life what truths and values you have decided to live up to, let your life tell you what truths you embody, what values you represent." Sharing stories of frailty and strength, of darkness and light, Palmer will show you that vocation is not a goal to be achieved but a gift to be received.

The first audio program from best-selling author Parker J. Palmer

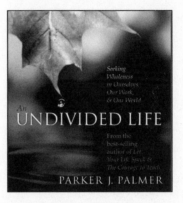

An Undivided Life

Seeking Wholeness in
Ourselves, Our Work,
and Our World

What does it mean to live "an undivided life"? For renowned educator and best-selling author Parker J. Palmer, it means living a life of authenticity in which "soul and role" are fully aligned. Now, this living legend—whose books have sold nearly one million copies to date—offers his first-ever audio program, *An Undivided Life.*

With heartwarming stories, insightful reflections, and poetic wisdom from his lifetime of work, this landmark journey gives listeners guidance and inspiration to deepen the journey toward wholeness, congruent with inner truth and aligned with the soul.

Spoken-Word Audio
Published by Sounds True
5 hours / 5 CDs
ISBN: 978-1-59179-362-5

Credits

GRATITUDES: Excerpt from "Stone" by D. M. Thomas in John Wain, ed., *Anthology of Contemporary Poetry: Post-War to the Present* (London: Hutchinson & Co., 1979), p. 27. Used by permission.

PRELUDE: From "The Future" published in *Stranger Music: Selected Poems and Songs* by Leonard Cohen © 1993. Reprinted with permission of McClelland & Stewart Ltd.

II: "As Once the Winged Energy of Delight," translated by Stephen Mitchell copyright © 1982 by Stephen Mitchell, from *The Selected Poetry of Rainer Maria Rilke* by Rainer Maria Rilke, translated by Stephen Mitchell. Used by permission of Random House, Inc.

Excerpt from "Someone Digging in the Ground," by Rumi in Coleman Barks and John Moyne, trans., *The Essential Rumi* (San Francisco: HarperSanFrancisco, 1995). Used by permission of Coleman Barks.

III: Excerpt from "Maybe," in *House of Light* by Mary Oliver. Copyright © 1990 by Mary Oliver. Reprinted by permission of Beacon Press, Boston.

Excerpt from "Little Gidding" in FOUR QUARTETS, copyright 1942 by T.S. Eliot and renewed 1970 by Esme Valerie Eliot, reprinted by permission of Harcourt, Inc. and by permission of Faber and Faber Limited.

IV: Excerpt from "Someone Digging in the Ground," by Rumi in Coleman Barks and John Moyne, trans., *The Essential Rumi* (San Francisco: HarperSanFrancisco, 1995). Used by permission of Coleman Barks.